REVOLUTIONARY LOVE:

FIND HEALING, FREEDOM, AND REST THROUGH THE POWER OF GOD'S LOVE

Copyright 2015 Scott Wessell

Corem Deo Publishing

Table of Contents

All It Takes It 3 Days...

In three days you can radically transform your relationthip with God!

Turn to page 151 for more information...

INTRODUCTION

Without a doubt, God's love is the most important truth to grasp. A loving and personal God is what separates Christianity from all other religions. All other gods are loveless taskmasters.

God's love is the foundation for all of life. In a very real way, God's love is more substantial and real than the chair you're sitting in right now. Everything that we know in life was built upon the foundation of His love.

But as important as it is, it's almost equally as difficult to get that profound truth from your head to your heart. I know this personally. I was raised in a broken home. I had an abusive stepfather who taught me things about love and God that seriously messed me up for decades.

One of the biggest lies I believed was that I needed to be punished when I sinned to reestablish my relationship with God. However, God wouldn't punish me and that made things even worse for me emotionally. I was so desperate for God's love that I decided that if He wasn't going to punish me that I would punish myself. So I made a whip and whipped my back until I couldn't stand it. It was black and blue for days. Once my guilt was assuaged, I felt like I could be close to God once again.

I know that you might be thinking, "Oh my, this man has some serious problems." If you had met me ten years ago, you would have been right. But God, in His grace, did a massive work in my life. He brought me to a place where I can correctly understand and experience His extraordinary love.

If you're reading this book, you probably have some issues with understanding or experiencing God's love too. I'm here to tell you that there is hope! I'm living proof of it.

What I discovered on my journey is that the real battle is in the mind. 2 Corinthians 10:4-5 says, "For the weapons of our warfare are not carnal but mighty in God for pulling down strongholds, casting down arguments and every high thing that exalts itself against the knowledge of God, bringing every thought into captivity to the obedience of Christ..." If you'll notice in this verse, all the weapons of war are used to fight an inner battle. They are used for pulling down strongholds in your life, casting down argument (or mindsets), and taking all of your thoughts captive to make them obedient to Christ.

It is my prayer that this book gives you weapons and tactics to wage a good war, win the battle of your mind, and remove the blockages that have kept you from God's love.

There is a simple formula to remember while you process this book: if you change what you think and change what you do, you will change how you feel. Read that again—it's very powerful if you put it to use.

Pastor Scott Wessell

THE PROBLEM—BROKENNESS

It never ceases to amaze me, the destruction that sin and the devil can cause. It doesn't matter if you have had a tough life or a great life; none of us are untouched by the deceitfulness of the enemy's schemes.

If your upbringing was hard and you suffered through some traumatic things, you're not surprised that you may have issues with God's love. It's often expected and you usually have some good ideas about why. On the other hand, if you're someone that has had a great upbringing and didn't suffer through traumatic events, you too can still have barriers regarding God's love. For this group of people, it's often harder to identify why because the cause is subtler.

But regardless of whether your past was good or bad, any issues or misunderstanding you might have with God's love started in your past. Something happened (usually multiple something's). Whether you experienced abuse or something as simple as not getting an emotional need met, that started a chain of events. You chose to perceive the event in a certain way. This, in turn, caused you to believe lies.

A classic case of this is a child with parents in the middle of a divorce. No loving parent would ever want to hurt their child or scar them in any way, but kids often unintentionally get caught in the crossfire of fighting parents. As a child, you have no grid to process all the volatile emotions in your parent's relationship.

Through your eyes, they can do no wrong. So you search your little brain for a cause, which inevitably ends up being yourself. You reason, "Mommy and Daddy are mad because something is wrong with me." No, Mommy and Daddy were being selfish and unloving towards each other and you had nothing to do with it. Now that you're grown up you might understand that, but the lies it formed in you have taken hold and shaped your interactions with God and with others.

That's really the most pernicious thing about lies. A lie can control your life even when you know it's a lie. You can know what lie you believe and you can even know the truth but sometimes you can still feel powerless against the lie. As I said in the beginning—the devil is a punk and has wreaked great destruction in all of our lives and the sticky nature of lies is one of his tricks that continues the destruction in our lives.

Regarding God's love, we have all believed lies that tell us that try to separate us from it. Lies that tell us we don't deserve it, that we are not worthy of it, that we will never be good enough for it, and that we have too many faults and shortcomings to be loved. Or we believe the lie that we have to earn God's love. We feel driven to do, do, do and go, go, go because we need to prove our worthiness.

Lies from the past also make us fearful. As a species, fear of rejection has a strangle hold on us, it's an outright pandemic within humanity. It causes us to either be needy and clingy, a people-pleaser or it causes us to reject before we are rejected—to push everyone away, including God, which leaves us in heartbreaking isolation.

Fear also creates an inability to trust God and to trust His love. Some of us hear that we have a heavenly

Father that loves us and it scares us—"I was 'loved' by my earthly father and it scared me. There's no way I'm going to let another Father love me again." So we keep our guard up, always on the defensive, keeping God a polite but safe distance from our heart of hearts.

The result of all of this is a serious lack of faith in God's love. We know all the bible verses, the songs, and the pithy quotes but no matter how hard we try we just can't seem to convince our hearts to trust Him. Sometimes we try to talk ourselves into trusting him but we bail out the second our stress levels rise.

So what's the solution? The answer is simple and at the same time very difficult. We need two things: to believe correctly—stop empowering the lies—and to experience correctly—start letting God become more real to us.

The rest of this book is formatted to do just that; challenge your beliefs and paradigms and give you some practical tools to help you experience more of His love. Each chapter starts with a Getting Ready exercise. It's designed to teach you how to experience God's presence. Also, every chapter ends with a Let's Get Real exercise. They are meant to be soul searching and challenging.

Some books can be read quickly this is not one of them. If you really want to get the most out of this book you need to slow down, do the exercises, and engage God. There are no medals for finishing the book in a couple of days but there will be a great reward for you if you internalize the principles in this book. I suggest reading one chapter a day. It's best if you can read it and do the exercises in one sitting but if you need to break it up you can do that too.

Lastly, before you more on to a new chapter, spend some time reviewing what God spoke to you in the previous ones.

THE SOLUTION—LOVE

God is love.

Three small words with great meaning. Love isn't something that God does; love is who He is. It is a part of His nature and character. To separate love from God would be like trying to separate your brain from your mind; if it were possible to separate them, each would cease to be what they are.

God is love.

1 Corinthians 13:4-8 is the Bible's description of love. Its intended purpose is to show us believers what our love for others should look like. It is a description of love, and because God is love, it is also a description of God's love.

If you have never looked at these verses from this perspective you're in for a treat. No longer will they remind you of how short you fall, but you will be amazed and see God's great love in new ways for the first time.

LOVE SUFFERS LONG

GETTING READY

From here on out, before you dive into each chapter, I'm going to walk you through a little quieting of your soul. Psalms 131:2 "Surely I have calmed and quieted my soul, like a weaned child with his mother; Like a weaned child is my soul within me."

Make sure you're someplace that you can focus, without distractions. Close your eyes and take a few deep breaths. Now, ask God to bless you with His presence. Just wait for a minute. You may feel a peace come over you, an inner sense of wellbeing, or even happiness.

Now ask God to open your heart to the truth of His love.

LONG SUFFERING

The love passage in 1 Corinthians 13 begins with the statement, "Love suffers long". It means what it sounds like. Love actively and willingly allows itself to suffer for great lengths of time.

One of the clearest pictures of suffering long is a small child playing with a docile dog. The child will grab the dog's ears and yank with all his might, he will yell with a high pitched voice in the dogs face, he will hit the dog repeatedly, climb on top of it, bounce up and down, and of course pull on its tail.

The poor dog, which is obviously suffering, just lies there doing nothing, taking the child's mistreatment without snapping, growling, or barking. The dog's response is the principle idea of suffering long, which is enduring "evil, injury, and provocation, without being filled with resentment, indignation, or revenge".[i] Just like the docile dog, love willingly endures and restrains itself from punishing those that offend it.

Because God is love, God suffers long. What does He suffer? God suffers the offences and insults that we are constantly hurling at Him with our rebellious and sinful choices. Every day, you and I choose our will over His, we choose happiness over holiness, we choose secret sins over purity of heart, and we reject Him. And God's response? In His willingness to suffer long with us, He is not filled with resentment, indignation, or revenge. He quietly endures and withholds the punishment that we deserve without getting upset.

Read that part again and ask God to help it sink in.

Some of this may be hard for you to believe, but even though we deserve to be punished and God would be blameless in exacting justice, He desires more for us. If He didn't, He wouldn't put up with us.

God created us for a reason and He desires us to experience Him the way we were created to—as our Father. Not only that, but He wants our experience of Him as Father to be to the same degree and extent that Jesus experiences Him as a father.

Think about that for a second: to what extent does Jesus experience God as Father?

Because He is committed to having a Father–child relationship with us, He willingly suffers our temporal insults so that we can enjoy His eternal treasures. He suffers because He wants to give us what we cannot give ourselves, and what's even crazier is that He does so without personal benefit. If that last sentence trips you up, don't worry. We'll deal with that thought more when we talk about how Love Does Not Seek It's Own.

God's willingness and ability to suffer should cause great joy in our hearts, because if God did not suffer for us, we would suffer for eternity. We should rejoice that God's ability to love exceeds our ability to sin and that all of our sins, as great as they seem to us, are as nothing in the vastness of God's love that suffers long.

But why? Why would God love me, and even more so, why would He love me like that? That's one of the most common questions I hear. We are desperate to figure out how something so amazing could be true. We approach His love like this: if we can wrap our minds around it then we will believe it and stop believing the lies.

Here's the deal, even if you understood His love and all the reasons why, it still wouldn't make a difference. Intellectual answers will never satisfy emotional questions. The reason we want to know why has nothing to do with a solid answer, but deep-seated feelings that the lies have produced in us.

That said I'm going to attempt to satisfy both for you.

The reason why God loves you and why He loves you in such an unbelievable way is because His love for you has nothing to do with you. I know all the insecurities probably come out when you read that, but stay with me for a second.

God loves you, because He is love not because of you. He loves because that is what He does and He has set his love on you. For all my performance based people out there, don't be sad by this! This is glorious news! If His love for us is not dependent on us that means… you are loved no matter what! You perform well… you are loved! You perform poorly… you are loved! No matter what, you are loved!

Let me explain this with a personal story. About four years ago, Aiden, my first child was born. I fell in love with him before he was even born and from the moment I saw him I experienced a kind of love for him that words cannot describe. But, for the first year of a baby's life, they are very needy, demanding, and not very thankful. The truth is, Aiden had no real concept of my love for him.

How did he repay me for my great love? Well, the third or fourth week of his life, I was in the middle of changing his diaper and he decided to baptize me with poop. Seriously, you'd be astonished if you knew how forceful human waste could exit such a tiny little bottom. But it didn't end there. He also threw up on me countless times, he ruined a few dress shirts, he peed on me, and the most challenging thing was that every two hours he woke me up screaming for food and another diaper change.

Make no mistake; having a newborn is hard, sleep depriving work.

But none of that changed my love for him. He was completely clueless about my great love for him and he did things that were not fun for me. But my love for him wasn't about what he could offer me. I loved him because I had set my heart on him even before I had met him.

17

There was and is nothing he can do to ever change my love for him. He has made me suffer and will continue to make me suffer and I receive it gladly. I receive it not because I'm a glutton for punishment, but because I possess a love for him larger than he will ever know or fully understand. I'm okay with that because my love isn't about his response to me; my love is about him.

In the same way, God set His love on you long before you were even born. His love is so profound that you will never know its depths. And because He loves you, He willingly suffers long with you, through all your junk, and never once regrets His choice to love you. He happily suffers, not so you can give Him something, but so He can give you something—His great love.

MAKING IT REAL

In this section I will be giving you different exercises to help you understand and experience the truths of God's love.

The purpose of this chapter's exercise is to, in a small way, see God's love for us from his perspective. So, take a moment to identify someone in your life that you have a profound love for. Let your mind dwell on them for a few moments. Let your love for them well up in your heart—think about all the things you adore about them.

Now, as you are in that state, imagine God feeling the same way towards you. Just sit in that space, feeling towards your loved one, and imagine God feeling the same towards you. Stay there as long as you can.

Take a few minutes and in the space provided below write down any insights or challenges you had with the exercise. If you were unable to emotionally connect with the exercise, that's okay. Talk to God about it. Tell Him why it was difficult. Don't try and be spiritual, just tell Him how you really feel.

For these exercises I recommend that if you find ones that really resonate with you practice them on a regular basis.

LOVE IS KIND

GETTING READY

Make sure you're in a place that you can focus without distractions. Close your eyes and take a few deep breaths. Repeat the exercise from the last chapter. Think about someone that you have a profound love for. Let your feelings well up inside you.

As you enjoy those feelings for that person, imagine God having those same feelings for you. Imagine His delight over you.

Thank God for His presence in this moment.

Now ask God to open your heart to the truth of His kindness.

LOVE IS KIND

The second characteristic of love is that it is "kind". Kindness, in its most basic sense, means to bless or benefit someone without thought of repayment. Some practical examples of everyday kindness would be helping a little old lady cross the street, holding an elevator for someone, or letting someone go before you in a check out line at the grocery store.

Three things must be present in order for an act to qualify as being kind. First, the act needs to bless someone else. Second, it needs to not directly benefit the one being kind. Third, there needs to be no expectation of repayment from the one doing the act.

For example, if a Boy Scout helps a little old lady cross a street that would be kind. But, if the Boy Scout helps the little old lady halfway across the street, then asks for money to help her cross the other half of the street, this would not be kind. The essence of kindness is to bless someone else with no personal benefit and no expectation of compensation. That is what God does.

So, not only does God, in His love, suffer long, endure mistreatment and insults without becoming resentful, but He also actively seeks out opportunities to bless and be a benefit to those who are offending him! So crazy, right? As we do stuff to insult and offend Him, He doesn't think about how He's going to get us back, but He dreams up ways to bless us!

It's important to remember the difference between a blessing and a reward. A reward is something that is earned, like a paycheck—there is nothing kind about an employer giving what is deserved. God's love does not reward you; it blesses you. A blessing is something that is not based on performance or behavior. It's like a gift to someone special just because you love them.

God, in His love, is kind towards us, which means that He actively seeks out opportunities to bless us. Take a moment and think about the implication of that statement. How many opportunities does a sovereign, omnipotent, infinite, creative God have to bless us?

God is not restrained in any way in His ability to bless—He actually creates and handcrafts opportunities for you to experience His kindness! But wait, it gets better! God does not bless us in accordance with who we are; He blesses us in accordance to who He is! His blessings are not contingent on our behavior. God does not bless us because we are good; He blesses us because He is good.

What does God ask for in return? NOTHING!

His desire is to bless us, not to burden us—He is seeking to do things for us, not to get things from us. Here is the cold, hard truth for the performer in you: You have nothing to give Him. There is nothing that you have that is not already His. Everything that you think you're doing for Him and giving to Him is His in the first place. He gave you the ability to do, and everything you give to Him He owns; every time you do or give, in reality God is giving to Himself.

God's remarkable kindness towards us should cause excessive thankfulness in us; our hearts should be overflowing with gratitude and gratefulness. God, in His kindness, showers us with blessings regardless of our actions or our attitudes! That should make your heart overflow with thankfulness.

But sometimes, instead of being thankful, we are skeptical. We want to know why. "Why in the world would God want to bless me regardless of how I act? That seems absurd." The concept can seem so foreign to us, but it shouldn't. Let me explain with another story about Aiden.

Now, normally what happens when women get pregnant is that they go through what is known as "nesting". They instinctively begin to prepare the "nest" for the new arrival. But my beautiful wife didn't have a chance to go into nesting mode because, well, I beat her to the punch.

I was so excited about my little baby boy that I began to go crazy preparing the house for him, but especially his room. At that time we lived in a condo and his room looked into the neighbors room. I couldn't have that. My baby needed a better view. So, I bought a vinyl window art covering. It was blue sky and puffy white clouds. It took me hours to cut and get it to stick without air bubbles in the pictures. I was determined that there would be no air bubbles. Not because I'm a perfectionist, but because it was for my baby. I wanted the puffy clouds and blue-sky window to look flawless for him.

Then there were the decorations. We had decided to go with a Noah's Ark theme. So, I painted and put wall decals up all around the room. Then the crib came and I spent a couple more hours putting it together.

All this was done with great anticipation. I was so eager to meet my little man and I wanted to create an environment for him that displayed my extravagant love for him. I knew that he would be oblivious to 99% of what I had labored for hours to give him, but I didn't care!

I wasn't concerned with him acknowledging everything I'd done. In truth, the room wasn't even about him—it was about my love for him. My heart's desire was that he would experience good from me, and my desire for him to experience good caused me to go over the top. I had an excessive love for him and I expressed it lavishly.

That is God's heart for you. He wants to bless you in accordance to how much He loves you. His desire is for you to experience good from Him. And you're going to be oblivious to most of it, but it's not about you. His blessings are about His love for you.

If I, an earthly father, desire to lavish good upon my child, how much more does your Heavenly Father desire to do the same?

The answer to "why" is because God desires you. He wants you. You are His favorite. He longs to be with you. If God had a fridge in heaven, your picture would be stuck to it.

Now, I understand that it might be hard to believe all that if you believe lies about your inadequacy and worthlessness. You might have spent a long time telling yourself that you are worthless. In fact, you've probably organized your life around that lie and it's a difficult thing to just walk away from all that.

See, one of the worst things about lies is that sometimes the truth upsets the delicate balance that has become our life. Believing the truth means that all we know and are comfortable with has to change. That can be a scary proposition. Sometimes we choose to stay in the brokenness that we are comfortable with instead of the healing that requires stretching.

I've got good news: you don't have to overhaul your entire life in a day. Baby steps are fine and in some cases, they are preferred. Our relationship with God in this life is about progress, not perfection.

So, how do you move forward and start believing this truth? The answer is both simple and difficult—accept it by faith. Even if it feels wrong or makes you uncomfortable, you choose to believe it anyway. Remember, feelings follow your thoughts and actions. Change your thoughts and you'll change your feelings!

MAKING IT REAL

Since your feelings follow your thoughts and actions let's take some time and evaluate your thoughts and actions (Write down your answer to each question in the spaces provided).

Think about your most common negative feelings regarding God's love for you. It might be feelings of worthlessness, fear of rejection, or a drive to perform. Whatever it is, what are the common thoughts that accompany those feelings? Be as detailed as possible.

Now, what are the actions or behaviors that you usually engage in when you are experiencing those feelings? Be as detailed as possible.

Now it's time to figure out what you should be thinking and doing to change those feelings. So, look at the list of thoughts that you created. Identify the ones that are based on lies (most of them probably are). Here comes the more challenging part: what are the truths for each lie that you typically think? Find a Bible verse for each truth.

Take a look at your list of actions and behaviors and walk through a similar process. Which behaviors are either unhealthy or unholy? Which behaviors are reactions to your feelings? Write down some alternative behaviors that are in line with the truths and Bible verses you just wrote down.

Okay, you've done a lot of thinking and writing. What's next? Well, that's where the rubber meets the road. Now you need to start thinking those things and doing those things. As you do, your feelings will begin to change towards God and His love for you. In order to help you do that, go back and write down when and where you will begin to implement your new thoughts and behaviors. Writing this part out will drastically improve your ability to implement them.

Don't expect this to be a silver bullet that will instantly transform you. It will take some practice and consistency. But if you put in the work, I guarantee that you will begin to notice a change.

To help set yourself up for success, keep this list in your Bible or put them in your phone (you can use an app like sticky notes and use the list as your lock screen). Review them frequently and pray over these truths daily.

LOVE DOES NOT ENVY

GETTING READY

Review the list of truths you created from the last chapter and make sure you're in a place that you can focus, without distractions.

Choose one of the truths from your list.

Close your eyes and take a few deep breaths. Now, thank God for that truth. Tell him how you'd like to be able to live more of it out. Now, take a few minutes and imagine what your life would look like if that truth sunk deeply into your heart. In faith, thank God for making that truth a reality in your life. This might feel fake or forced at first, but be honest with God. If you can't thank Him as if the truth is a reality in your life, at least talk to Him about how you'd like it to be a reality.

Take a few deep breaths and ask God to bless this time with Him. Ask Him to open up your heart to what He wants to speak to you through this next chapter.

LOVE DOES NOT ENVY

The best way to describe envy is malicious jealousy. Jealousy causes a desire to have something that belongs to someone else. You see someone with the newest iPhone and you look at your flip phone and start to feel gadget jealously. You think to yourself, "I just have to get one of those!" Envy is a little different. Instead of creating a desire to have, it causes a desire to see what someone else has taken from them. At the heart of envy is resentment; it is not so much the thought of "I want what they have" but one of "they don't deserve what they have".

An example of envy in everyday life can be seen in unrequited love. You have a crush on someone and are pining for them. You make the mistake of telling your friend who, before you are able to muster the courage to confess your undying love, begins to date your "true love". Besides betrayal, you feel envy; you start to entertain thoughts that your friend doesn't deserve someone so special and you begin to secretly, or not so secretly, hope your friend gets dumped so they will experience the heartache you are.

The essence of envy is being grieved at the good that others enjoy and having ill will towards them.[ii] Another great example of envy is the Occupy Wall Street Movement. At the heart of the movement was an anger over the blessings that the 1% had in their life. Crowds gathered demanding that the 1% should be punished— AKA take their blessings from them.

The good news is that love does not envy, which means that love is not grieved at the good in our lives and has no ill will towards us.

Because God is love, God does not envy. But what does God do? You see, when you are describing something you can do it in two ways. One way is in the form of an attribution; you make a positive statement regarding it. Example: Love is kind. It tells you a positive attribute that love possesses. It also implies that love does not posses the opposite quality of kindness, which would be rudeness.

33

The second way you can describe something is in the form of a negation; you make a negative statement about it. Example: Love does not envy. It tells you a negative attribute that love does not possess. But it also implies that love possesses the opposite quality of envy.

So what's the opposite of envy? What's the opposite of not being grieved over good things in people's lives and not having ill will towards them? The opposite of ill will is good will and the opposite of being grieved over good in someone's life is to be excited and happy.

God, in His love, does not envy, which means that He is our biggest advocate, not our biggest critic; He does not stand over us and criticize, but stands beside us and supports us. You see, envy comes from a heart of resentment and criticism. God has neither towards us.

Take a moment and let that thought sink in—God has no resentment or criticism towards you.

People that experience envy have an emotional commitment of ill will towards others. They earnestly desire to see bad happen to someone. God also has an emotional commitment, but it's the opposite emotional commitment from someone who is envious. His emotional commitment is good will towards us; His earnest desire is to see good happen to us.

Can you believe that? God is emotionally committed to our success, not to our failure—He sees our success as His success, our promotion as His promotion, the good that happens to us as good that happens to Him. Why? Because He has forever bound His heart with our hearts and when you experience an emotion, He experiences the same emotion.

When you hurt, He hurts. When you feel rejected, He feels that with you. When you're happy, He is happy with you. When you rejoice, He rejoices with you. His heart is tied to yours.

Sometimes we forget that God is emotionally committed to our good; we forget that He is our greatest supporter. When too much good happens in our life, we start to get nervous, we hold our breath, and wait for the "other shoe to drop". We think that God doesn't want us to experience too much good, so we wait for something bad to happen; we wait for God to be envious.

But that mindset is a misunderstanding of who God is; it assumes that God wants to limit His goodness in our lives and that He wants us to suffer. God has absolutely no desire to see us suffer and He has zero interest in limiting the good that we experience. God is good and it is flat out against God's nature to limit good. To say that God wants to limit the good we experience in our lives is the same as saying that God wants to limit our experience of Him. This is a lie from the pit of hell!

God wants to lavish, not limit, the good in our lives. The reason He wants to shower us with good is because He is emotionally committed to us. He has bound His emotional well-being with ours; when we suffer He suffers and when we rejoice He rejoices. God is joyful, not resentful, about the good in our lives.

We don't deserve it, but He wants us to have it anyway, and there is no limit to good that a limitlessly good God has to give us!

Once we realize that God is our greatest advocate it should cause a great sense of peace in us. We can trust God; He is not grieved with the good in our lives and has no ill will towards us. We can rest in the knowledge that God is not looking to take anything from us and His only desire is to bless us.

I know that for some of us, it is difficult to see God as an advocate, not a critic. After all, isn't the Father angry and doesn't He want to punish us. Isn't that why Jesus is our advocate? Doesn't Jesus protect me from my angry, critical Heavenly Father?

The short answer is "no". No one in the Trinity is critical of you—Jesus isn't critical, the Holy Spirit isn't critical, and the Father isn't critical either.

Viewing God as critical is to believe a lie. But you probably know that already. The question is, why do you think of God as critical even if you know it's not who He is? Most likely, you can trace it back to your upbringing. Someone was critical of you and you never felt like you could meet their standard. You probably learned to be highly critical of yourself too, and maybe even critical of others.

The bottom line is that if you view God as critical, He is probably not the only critical voice in your life. In reality, the criticism you feel from "God" is actually all the voices from your past.

So, how do you overcome living under the weight of criticism? It all starts by understanding what criticism is. At its heart, criticism is a lack or absence of grace.

There is a great saying: "You can't get out of your situation with the same mentality that you used to get yourself into it." The same is true with criticism. You cannot free yourself from criticism by staying in the hole that it dug for you. You need a new tool, a new paradigm, and that paradigm is grace.

What that means is that the normal efforts to escape a mentality, a habit, or sin doesn't work. Usually we spend all our time, energy and effort focusing on the thing we are trying to stop doing. In the case of criticism, we try to criticize ourselves out of being critical, and we fail to see the irony in that! The answer is simple: instead of focusing on what we shouldn't be doing, thinking, or feeling, we should be focusing on what we *should be* doing, thinking, or feeling. It's a focus on cultivating positive things, not a focus on stopping negative things.

So, what does that look like for criticism? Focus on grace. Being gracious to others and being gracious to yourself. And—this is a big one—focus on receiving grace from others. That last one is often an important one because our relationships with others affect our relationship with God. If you can learn to accept grace from others, it will help counteract the lies that God is critical instead of gracious with you.

Now, all this is great in theory, but the practice can actually be quite challenging. But it all goes back to the fact that your feelings follow your thoughts and actions. Your mind is the battlefield and you need to start fighting there with a winning strategy. Use the list of truths and behaviors you created in the last chapter and don't stop using that technique until grace begins to be your default for life.

MAKING IT REAL

God is emotionally committed to your well-being. He is your biggest supporter, your most fanatic fan. He has no desire to beat you down or be critical of you. The following exercise is designed to help you "see" things from God's point of view.

Think about someone in your life that you love deeply, someone that you are emotionally committed to their well-being. When you see them hurt, it breaks your heart. When you see them happy, it brings joy to your soul.

Think on them for a minute and let your heart fill up with affection for them. What do you really love about them? What's your favorite thing to do with them?

Now, what would you feel if they were hurting, if something terrible happened, and their world fell apart? What are you feeling for them? Imagine God feeling the same way for you whenever bad things happen to you. What does that evoke in you? Take a few minutes and talk to God about it. Write down your insights below.

Now, think again on your loved one. What would you feel if something amazing happened in their life, something that meant the world to them? What feelings are you experiencing for them? Imagine God feeling the same way for you when you experience His goodness. What does that evoke in you? Take a few minutes and talk to God about it. Write down your insights below.

If you were unable to connect with this exercise, that's okay. Just be honest with God. Tell Him that you'd like to believe that He feels a certain way towards you and do the best you can.

LOVE DOES NOT PARADE ITSELF

GETTING READY

Settle yourself in a place where you can focus and without distractions. Turn off your phone if you need to. Are there any lessons that resonated with you that you'd like to spend some more time on? If you want to, you can go back and redo an exercise or review a concept.

Close your eyes and take a few deep breaths. Begin to thank God for His presence. Ask him to increase the sense of His presence in this moment. Quiet your heart and take a few minutes to wait on God. As God's presence begins to settle on you, you might feel a peace come over you, an inner sense of well being, or even joy. Just spend some time enjoying God's presence.

Now, lift up this time to Him, ask Him to bless it and to open your heart wide to the truths He wants to teach you.

LOVE DOES NOT PARADE ITSELF

The next attribute of love in 1 Corinthians 13 is that "love does not parade itself". What does that mean? Well, to understand the meaning of this phrase, we first have to look at the purpose of a parade. The purpose of a parade is to be seen and to be the center of attention; it is a time to show off and gain recognition. There are no private parades. No one would participate in a parade if nobody showed up to watch—that would cease to be a parade and just become a lonely walk down the street.

When Paul says that love does not parade itself, that means that love is not looking to be the center of attention. Love does not exalt itself over others, it doesn't show off, and it isn't vying to be center stage.

At its heart, parading is about image. It's about being seen by others in a certain light. Those that parade themselves typically want to be seen as smart, competent, hardworking, attractive, or cool, etc. The list goes on and on.

But God does not parade Himself, which means that He is not concerned with image. If He is not concerned with image, then what is He concerned with? He is concerned with relationship, but not just any kind of relationship. He is concerned with a specific type of relationship—He wants us to experience Him as a Father.

Because His desire is to be a Father to us, in His love, the center of the universe allows us to be the center of attention. Read that last part again. The truth is that God deserves to be the center of everything. He is the only one worthy of attention, but in His great humility and care for us, He lets us take center stage in the relationship. You don't believe me? Here is a quick question that proves my point: who is the main focus of your prayers?

You might have a negative reaction to the answer to that question. You might be tempted to go into self-depreciating mode: "You're right, I'm such a self-obsessed loser!" But before you take a ride on that train, let me tell you a story.

When my first child, Aiden, was born, it was my first interaction with an infant. I had no idea what to expect. He was my first everything—first diaper change, first time burping a baby, etc. During that season, one thing was impressed upon me deeply: how helpless he was. Literally, a newborn will die if care is not given to them. Aiden was completely incapable of providing for any of his needs. And my wife's life and my life changed big time. Everything began to revolve around caring for this new precious gift God had given us. His eating cycle determined our activities as a family, His sleep cycle determined our sleeping patterns, and His needs came before our needs.

Just as God is the center of the universe, I am the head of my house. Just as we are 100% dependent on God to keep living, Aiden was 100% dependent on my wife and I to live. Now, I could have demanded that Aiden give me the respect due my position in the family. I could have required him to acknowledge his dependence on me. My wife and I were the center of his universe. It was by our good pleasure that he ate, slept, and had his needs met.

Even though we were the center of Aiden's universe, we, in our great love for him, allowed him to occupy the center of our attention. Every time he made a sound, everything in the house stopped and we listened to the cute little sounds he made. Every time he cried, we would jump up to meet whatever need he was requesting to be met. We lavished him with our attention because we were concerned with him experiencing our love and we had no desire for him to recognize our position.

Just as my wife and I were the center of Aiden's universe but we eagerly made him the center of our attention, so too God is the center of the universe but joyfully makes you the center of His attention. Why? Because God's primary concern is that we experience His love. Just like my wife and I did with our son, God lavishes you with His attention and affection.

You are the center of God's attention, you are the center of the relationship, and God would have it no other way! He delights in putting you at the center of the relationship and keeping you at the center of His attention!

So, if God doesn't parade Himself, what does He do? Well, the opposite of parading is humility. Humility is an essential quality of God's love. Humility is what causes Him to put the center of attention on others.

In His humble love, God lowers Himself in order to raise us up. Let that thought sink in. The God of the universe, the all-powerful one, lowered Himself by becoming one of us, serving us, and dying for us with one purpose—to lift us up.

God's focus is raising you up not to raise Himself up. God's love focuses outside of Himself—He does not try to be seen as great, but instead He makes others great.

God is the epitome of humility. He does not parade Himself, but He lowers Himself. Knowing that should cause us to realize that God's attention is eagerly focused on us; He is attentive towards us. Your Father is lovingly watching over you. Because He is so mindful and attentive of you, you should be persuaded that He hears you, that He has turned His ear to hear your cry, and that He is actively doing something to meet your needs.

You can rest assured that you are not going unnoticed by your Father—in His great humility, He sees you and He cares for you.

For some, this is too much to believe, especially for those with a low view of themselves. After all, how can

God, who is so perfect, be eager to make me the center of attention when I am so messed up?

This thinking, seeing yourself as worthless, is based on lies. It's a mentality that places more credence on our perspective than God's. It's a point of view that says that God must convince me if His perspective differs from mine. I know that we probably don't actually say that to God, but when we refuse to believe what He says about us and get stuck on the "why" that's exactly what we do.

Feelings of worthlessness are based on a lie that God has somehow miss-valued us, that we have a more accurate view of reality than God does. Now, the challenge is to not let these truths feed into your feelings of worthlessness.

For some reason because we can't understand why God would love us, we tell ourselves it can't be true. But the reality is, there are a lot of things in life that we don't understand, like thermal nuclear dynamics or quantum physics, which we believe because an expert told us it's true.

So, what's the real reason that we don't believe the expert on love, God? It boils down to emotional commitment. We are emotionally committed to thinking certain things about ourselves and no matter what God says, we are more emotionally committed to the lies of our past than the truth of God's love.

This brings up a very important aspect about lies. Lies don't need to be believed to influence you. Or, in other words, you can know that a lie is a lie and it can still have a powerful effect on you. I learned this first hand about ten years ago. Growing up, I was told that I was stupid. My step-dad told me I was an idiot, and because of a learning disability, I was pulled from normal classes and put into special education classes. School confirmed what my step dad had been telling me all along.

Eventually, I realized that I'm not stupid. I actually have a very quick and clever mind. But the lie that I'm stupid caused me to see the world from a certain perspective. It affected the way I interacted with people. It influenced my drive in life. Even though I knew I wasn't stupid, my perspective and my mode of relating to people was still based on that lie.

It didn't happen overnight, but once I realized that a lot of my life was organized around a lie, I began to reshape my life to fit the truth. I changed how I interacted with others, I changed my "worthless" paradigms, and I gave up my "why bother trying?" attitude.

How did I do all that? I stopped listening to myself and I started talking to myself. I stopped listening to the lies and the thought patterns that were based on lies and I started telling myself the truth.

This is one of the most powerful things you can do to overcome the effect of lies on your life. What does it look like? First, you need to identify a thought that is influenced by a lie. Then you call it what it is—a lie. Next you attach truth to it. You tell yourself, "No, that is a lie and this is the truth. I am choosing to believe the truth."

I want to share one more thing that will really make this even more powerful. At one time, when I was in the throws of lies about my identity and my self-worth, I had a life-changing encounter with God. He spoke to me clearly and powerfully; He told me that He wasn't going to take away my identity issues, but that I needed to give them to Him. I did just that, and something broke that night. A stronghold that had wielded tyrannical power was toppled with a single act: me refusing to hold onto my identity of brokenness.

What is true for me is also true for you. The reason lies can have such a powerful effect on us even when we don't want them to is because we're not letting them go. We don't reject them. We create space for them to still function in our heads and hearts.

So when you practice the tool above, you need to do more than call the lie a lie and attach truth to it. There needs to be within you a rejection of the lie. You're heart should respond by saying, "NO! That is a lie. It is not who I am. I reject that! This is the truth of who I am…"

To really give this exercise some teeth, let's spend some time prepping ourselves. What is one of the biggest lies in your life? What is the truth regarding yourself, God, and that lie? What is one Bible verse that really speaks to you regarding the truth?

MAKING IT REAL
Now that you have identified a big lie in your life, know the truth to combat that lie, and have scripture to back up the truth; it's time to get real with yourself.

This is an exercise to help you stop listening to yourself and to start talking to yourself. What I'm about to ask you to do may seem kind of weird, but I want to encourage you to give it a shot anyway. Step out of your comfort zone and see what happens.

Go to a private place with a mirror: your bathroom or bedroom is ideal. As a side note, this exercise might take a while, so do it at a time when you won't be rushed. Now, as you look directly into your own eyes and tell yourself the lie you believe is a lie, tell yourself that you fully reject it, and that it is not a part of who you are anymore. Then, tell yourself the truth; the truth about how God views you, the truth about who you are in Christ, and the truth of what the Bible says. Tell yourself that you are choosing to believe the truth instead of the lie.

Now here's the one caveat. You have to really mean it when you say it. So, you might be staring at yourself in the mirror for a while before you can say it with conviction. If it takes a few days or weeks before you can do it and mean it, that's okay. The goal is progress, not perfection.

Do this exercise everyday until you don't need to do it any more. When is that, you ask? When you believe the truth and the lies don't have a hold on you anymore.

After you've done this exercise, write down your reaction to it. What was hard about it? What was easy about it? What thoughts went through your head while doing the exercise? What things were you feeling?

Now spend some time talking to God about what you just wrote.

LOVE IS NOT PUFFED UP

GETTING READY

Settle yourself in a place where you can focus and without distractions. Turn off your phone if you need to. Are there any lessons that resonated with you that you'd like to spend some more time on? If you want to, you can go back and redo an exercise or review a concept.

Close your eyes and take a few deep breaths. Think for a moment on some of the reasons that you love God and why you're thankful for Him in your life.

Now, take ten deep breaths. As you inhale, think the word "Father". As you exhale, either think or softly say, "I love You because/for Your…"

Next, spend some time just enjoying God and His presence.

LOVE IS NOT PUFFED UP

The next characteristic of love is that it "is not puffed up". Literally, love is not inflated with self-importance. To better understand what puffed up means, picture a balloon. It's a simple piece of rubber that when puffed up can become five to six times its original size. Puffing up is also seen in the animal world. It's what cats do before they fight: they arch their back, make their fur stand on end, and try to make themselves appear as big as possible.

For us, "puffed" up carries the connotation of making yourself as big as possible, inflating our sense of importance. The world and our lives are filled with people that are puffed up, people that think they are more special, more important, and more deserving than they really are.

Love, however, does not enlarge itself; it does not have an inflated sense of self-importance; it does not make itself bigger than it really is, nor does it assume a posture of arrogance. There is no disconnect between what love is and how it views itself.

In the previous chapter we covered the characteristic that love "does not parade itself". If you will remember, the key concept to parading was being the center of attention. Being puffed up and parading oneself are two sides to the same coin—pride. Parading is about outward action (how others see you) and being puffed up is about inner attitude (how you see yourself).

A common trait of those that are puffed up is their treatment of others. Because the self-important are filled with selfish ambition and conceit they have a nasty habit of lowering others in order to raise themselves up. The puffed up are fixated on titles and positions. They need to feel better than everyone else, so they often put others down, judging and criticizing them. They joke about them and make fun of them, bashing them with sarcasm.

God is not puffed up; He does not have an exaggerated or inflated sense of self-importance. Which means He does not lower us in order to raise Himself. God is not filled with selfish ambition or conceit. He does not put us down, He does not criticize us, He does not make fun of us, nor does He bash us with sarcasm. Because God is humble, the opposite is true—God thinks highly of us and holds us in high esteem. He raises us up, affirms us, encourages us, and genuinely cares for us.

Realizing that God is not puffed up should cause us to realize that God is not using us to feel better about Himself. We do not stroke His ego and we are not His trophies. The only thing He desires is for us to experience the love that He offers us. Once the significance of that thought sinks in, the proper response for us is to join the Psalmist and say, "Such knowledge is too wonderful for me, too great for me to understand!" (Psalm 139:6 NLT).

But sometimes it's hard to believe that about God, that He doesn't treat you bad to make Himself feel good, because so many people in our lives did just that. For some of us, there were important people in our lives who should have protected us, but instead they hurt us.

Growing up, I was traumatized and carried some deep wounds. I lived under a heavy cloud of darkness and depression. My favorite Bible character at that time was Jeremiah, the weeping prophet. His life was hard, full of heaviness and mourning, and he was called to a ministry of futility. Now, that's not an entirely accurate representation of Jeremiah, but that was my filter of brokenness. In many ways, I saw my own life in the pages of Jeremiah, that God had called me to a hard life that would be full of sorrow.

How do you grow through your past wounds and have a healthy outlook about life and God? There are three things you need to be. You need to be honest with yourself, you need to be open with others and God, and you need to be at peace with what has happened

Being honest with yourself. Sometimes the past causes us not to be as honest with ourselves as we should be. We play down the impact that it is having in our lives and we tell ourselves, "It's not that big of a deal. Other people suffer far worse things. I have no right to be upset about it. I just need to get over it." We deny that we are bitter or blame others or God for what happened. We sometimes will tell ourselves it's our fault. This is especially true if something happed to you as a child. Often we don't have the emotional intelligence to see things as they really are and we assign the blame to ourselves.

Being open with others and God. There is one thing I have consistently noticed over the years between those that have suffered trauma and are well adjusted and those that are stuck in the pain of their past. That one thing is processing. Those that process their painful memories are consistently better adjusted than those that ignore and stuff their painful memories.

Processing the painful memories is what being open is all about. Being open with others and with God. I know that might scare you because you're so used to stuffing your emotions and being "strong" that opening up to yourself is hard, let alone opening up to others and God.

Here's why you have to open up to someone besides yourself: God created you as a relational being. All your needs are designed to be met within the context of relationships, not in isolation. If you refuse to open up and let people love you in your pain, you are ensuring that you will be trapped in the pain of your past.

So, if you want to heal, you need to open up to the people in your life and to God. What does that look like? Being vulnerable. Letting them know how hard it is to live like you're living. Let them know where your pain comes from. Let them know what you think and feel about it. Basically, you need to let everything you have been stuffing out.

You don't need to let it all out in a day. You actually won't be able to. But you need to open the door and shine some light on those secret areas. If you're mad at God, let Him know. Cry. Yell. Be open with Him. Let Him into those deep areas. If you blame Him for what happened, let Him know. Work through that with Him. Blaming God for things becomes an invisible wall that often keeps us from experiencing the healing we desperately want.

Being at peace with what happened. The ultimate goal is to be at peace with what happened to you. That does not mean that you are approving of it or that you are forgetting it. It doesn't take away the pain, but it frees you from the bondage it has on you. One of the biggest traps we can get caught in regarding our past is asking, "Why?" Here is the truth—some "Why" questions will never be answered and chasing after the answer will only keep you stuck in the pain of the past.

Instead of searching for the "Why" ask yourself, "What's next?" This helps you come to peace with it. You cannot change what happened. You probably won't even be able to figure out why it happened. But you can move on from it in a productive way.

MAKING IT REAL

Let's put being honest and open into practice and learn to come to a place a peace with the bad stuff that's happened to you in life. This might take you a little while to get through, but I promise that it will be worth it.

Being honest: What do you really feel? What actually happened? Who do you hate because of it? Who do you blame because of it? What things have you done as a result that you deeply regret? What's the real impact of it in your life? How is it affecting your life and relationships now?

Be open: Write down some names of people you can begin to open up with.

Now, using the list you just created on the pervious page, answer the following questions: When will you open up to them? What are you going to open up to them about? How will you bring up the subject?

What do you need to be open with God about? Are you blaming Him for your past? Pull up an empty chair next to you. Imagine God is sitting there. How close do you want the chair to you? What position do you want it to be in relation to you: in front of you or beside you?

As you imagine God sitting in the chair, tell Him what you need to say. Don't worry about being "spiritual" or offending Him. Be open with Him about the things that are deep in your heart.

Write down any insights or challenges that come out of your time talking to God.

Be at peace: To help your past do something besides hurt. Take some time and journal about this question: "What are the pearls of wisdom I can take away from this painful memory?"

If you are caught up on "why" questions, spend some time surrendering those questions and ask God, "What's next?" Take some time and journal about this.

LOVE IS NOT RUDE

GETTING READY

Settle yourself in a place that you can focus without distractions. Turn off your phone if you need to. Are there any lessons that resonated with you that you'd like to spend some more time on? If you want, you can go back and redo an exercise or review a concept.

I'm about to share with you one of my favorite ways to calm myself and quite my mind before I spend time with the Lord. Of course, you are welcome to substitute this, or any other "Getting Ready" exercise with a previous one that really resonated with you or any other preferred routine you may have.

Close your eyes and take a few deep breaths. While still breathing slowly and deeply, read the following either out loud or to yourself.

Be still and know that I am God
Be still and know that I am
Be still and know
Be still
Be

LOVE IS NOT RUDE

Love "does not behave rudely". To understand this characteristic of love, we first have to understand what rudeness is. Rudeness is a thoughtless pursuit of a personal desire, regardless of the effect on others. The two components involved in rudeness are self-satisfaction and a disregard for others.

A great example of rudeness that we all experience from time to time happens in a busy parking lot, maybe during Christmas shopping season. You are driving around a full parking lot, looking for an empty space when you see someone packing their car with their recently purchased goods. You patiently wait for them with your signal on, indicating your intention to occupy the space after they leave. But then something rude happens: the car you are waiting for doesn't back out the way you expected them to and as you are waiting for them to get out of your way, another car rushes in and takes your spot. If you are particularly bold, you politely tell them that they took your parking spot, but they either ignore or have some not-so-kind words for you as they walk off to shop.

The reason these despicable parking spot thieves are rude is because they pursue their desire without thought of how their actions will affect you. But because Love does not behave rudely, it does not pursue its own desires without first considering how it will affect you.

God, in His love, is not rude towards us. He does not pursue His own desires to the exclusion of ours. The opposite is actually true: His desires are inclusive of our needs—He incorporates our needs into what He desires, which means He does not engage in actions that benefit Himself at our expense. While rudeness is quick to sacrifice others' needs for personal benefit, God is not rude and therefore we are not sacrificed on the altar of His personal benefit. But God goes beyond that: not only does He choose not to sacrifice you for His benefit. He actually does the opposite: He sacrifices Himself for your benefit!

The opposite of rudeness is thoughtfulness, which is what God is. How is God thoughtful? God does not move to action before thorough evaluation of our situation; He is not thoughtless towards our needs—He carefully considers our concerns. He takes into account the effect each of His actions will have on us. He thinks on us before He moves in the world around us. After much consideration, He chooses only that which is best for us.

You might have an issue with that last statement, that God has only done what's best for you. The big issue is, "Who is defining good?" From a limited perspective, what we see as good is not always what God sees as good from His eternal perspective. The difference comes from the final goal. God has a very different goal for us than what we have for ourselves.

God's goal is that we have the best eternity imaginable. Our goal is usually that we have the best life imaginable. Here is the truth: God has given you the best life possible in order to give you the best eternity imaginable. Everything, including the things you don't think of as good, God has allowed so that you could have the best eternity available.

Once we understand that God does not behave rudely, we can trust Him with our past and our future. Instead of holding onto our past, we can let go of it, knowing that God carefully considered what was best for us before He created us. Like Joseph, we can look back on our past, even the bad parts and say, "[Others in my life] intended to harm me, but God intended it all for good. He brought me to this position so I could save the lives of many people" (Genesis 50:20 NLT). Additionally, because God is thoughtful toward us, we don't have to be anxious about our future. Whatever the future brings, God has carefully considered what is best for us.

Trust is a difficult thing for a lot of us. One thing I consistently heard as I was doing research was that a lack of trust was one of the biggest hindrances to experiencing God's love. What's crazy is that knowing you have trust issues doesn't seem to do anything about our trust issues. There is almost a quiet resignation that says our inability to trust is unfixable. We decide to live with our lack of trust, try to get by and make due as best we can, knowing we will never be able to fully experience all that God has for us, because we just can't seem to muster up the ability to trust Him.

How do you get out of that rut? Well, the first thing to realize is that you don't actually have a trust issue… you have a control issue. You don't trust because you refuse to relinquish your control. And the real dilemma you've been trying to figure out is how can I talk myself into trusting God without losing control. The answer is, you can't. That's why you're stuck. You've decided that control is more important to you than experiencing God's promises.

To help your trust issue, we need to back it up one more step, because control is not the cause. It's a reaction to something—fear. Whenever we feel unsafe, we naturally attempt to exert control over people and over our environment. We learned this through life. All the bad things that happen to us are things that were outside of our control. Someone abused you and you couldn't do anything to stop them. Someone withheld their love and affection from you and there was nothing you could do to get them to love you. You lost a loved one and experienced feelings of helplessness.

Fear and a compulsion to control are the real issues that try to convince you that trust doesn't work. You need to focus on the root of the problem. Tackle this by addressing the fear and addressing the need for control.

First, let's look at the fear. Ask yourself, "What am I so afraid of regarding trusting God?" Next, ask yourself, "Why am I so afraid of that happening?" For example, a common answer to the first question is something like, "I'm afraid that God will let me down." Well, the next question is: why? What you're trying to discover is what you're really afraid of. So a common answer to, "Why am I afraid of God letting me down?" is "Because that will confirm that I am worthless and I don't want to put myself in that position." Well, now we can work on something like that! So, what is the real reason you're afraid to trust God? What's the deep down fear that is driving it all?

The next step is to address your need to control. One of the biggest truths to have in place is that control is an illusion. It's really something we tell ourselves to make us feel better. The reality is that there is very little that we actually control. The only things we can truly control are our moral choices, our attitudes, and our reactions to others. Other than that, we really can't control other people and we really can't control circumstances. They are mostly out of our hands. You are in control of yourself and that is it.

Take a moment and let yourself know that you really don't have as much control as you think you do.

The second step of overcoming a need to control is understanding what it does to others. When we try to control others, we are actually doing to them what we are most fearful of ourselves—not being in control. It actually creates unhealthy and codependent relationships, in which each person agrees that they will control the other person. We have a secret pact that says, "I will let you control me if you let me control you." That is not a relationship you want to be in. If you have control issues you are damaging the people in your life by removing empowerment from them. You are guilty of the thing you are most fearful of. Let that one sink in.

The third step is to take baby steps. Release control in small ways at first with those around you and with God. On an interesting side note, your relationship with others affects your relationship with God and vice versa. So if you want to grow in your ability to trust God, one practical way to begin to do that is to start trusting others—let go of the control.

Things don't have to be done in the exact way you want them to be done. The world will not come to an end if the pantry isn't organized "correctly". No one will die if your significant other gets to make a decision for themselves.

As you take baby steps, you will realize that you don't need to control as much as you thought. You see, we learn to control, because it made us feel safe. It is our defense mechanism, it's how we cope with life and make sense of the world. But now that you're saved, the thing that at one time helped you, now hinders you. The coping mechanisms that protected you when you lived in the kingdom of darkness are now wreaking havoc in your life now that you are a part of the kingdom of light.

MAKING IT REAL
Trusting that God has your best interest at heart can sometimes be a difficult thing to see, especially if your past or present is difficult. Sometimes we need to declare the truth to ourselves in spite of what we are feeling, and by

faith choose to believe God regardless of what our
experiences tell us.

In the space below, write out a prayer of confession
to God regarding your life. Declare to Him and yourself
that you believe that He has your best interest in mind
whenever He acts in your life. If you need to, list out the
hard things that have happened to you and in faith tell
Him that you believe that even those things, He is working
out for your good.

Now, here's where it might get difficult. When you sit
down to write this letter, don't get up until you have
written it, but don't write it until you can believe what
you're writing. It may be easy for you to do that, but it also
may take you a few hours of wrestling with God before
you can.

If it takes you a while, remember when Jacob wrestled the
angel, which was Jesus, in Genesis 32. He wrestled all night
long and refused to let go until God blessed him. If you've
got serious issues experiencing God's love, this can be a
big exercise for you. Wrestle with God and don't let go
until you can confidently say that everything in your life is
marked by God's goodness, even the painful stuff.

Dear God,

LOVE DOES NOT SEEK ITS OWN

GET READY

Well, if you've made it this far, you must be a glutton for punishment. I know that some of the topics I'm dealing with are heavy and difficult. You might even have been tempted to put the book down because I've asked you to walk though some tough heart-wrenching exercises. I'm proud of you for making it this far and I want to encourage you to keep going. There is no growth that occurs without difficulty and effort. To walk the easy path is to never change for the better. Keep pressing in and moving forward with the Lord.

Settle yourself in a place that you can focus and without distractions. Turn off your phone if you need to. Are there any lessons that resonated with you that you'd like to spend some more time on? If you want to, you can do go back and redo an exercise or review a concept.

Close your eyes and take a few deep breaths. Invite the Holy Spirit to lead you and guide you in this time. Thank God for His nearness and His presence.

Spend a few minutes waiting on the Lord. Wait for His presence to fill you from your head to your feet. You might feel a peace come over you, an inner sense of well-being, or even happiness.

Now, lift up this time to Him, ask Him to open your heart to the truths He wants to show you.

LOVE DOES NOT SEEK ITS OWN

There is a similarity between Love not behaving rudely and Love not seeking its own. Because love does not behave rudely, it considers others before it acts, and because love does not seek its own, it is not looking to meet its own needs. So, not only does love consider others before it acts. It is also unmotivated by selfish desires—they are two sides of the same coin.

A modern example of not seeking its own would be an altruistic deed, like giving a homeless man the change in your pocket as you walk by. In that act, you are giving without getting anything in return—it was completely selfless not seeking personal advantage or profit. Because love does not seek its own, it is selfless, it does not demand or desire its own advantage or profit, and it does not try to advance its position or better its situation.

Because God is love, God does not seek His own, which means that God is not looking to advance His position or better His situation. Indeed, it is impossible for God to do either because He is immutable and self-sufficient. Because God is immutable, He does not change, grow, or improve—God remains the same. If He were to seek personal benefit that would mean that He went from not having a benefit to having one. To do that requires change and change is something that God does not do. The second reason God does not seek His own is because He is also completely self-sufficient. He is not in need of, nor dependent on anything outside of Himself—He is lacking nothing. If God were to seek His own, that would imply that He is lacking in someway and needs to add something to who He is. God does not seek His own because He already has everything.

In practical terms, that means that God gains nothing from us. We do not add to the quality of His existence in any way, and we have nothing to give Him. God is in no way self-seeking in His relationship with us, not even in the slightest. The opposite of seeking personal benefit is seeking other's benefit, which is what God does for us. The reality is that we are the only ones that profit from our relationship with Him. God gains nothing from us, yet gives everything to us. He only gives, always gives, and forever gives and we only take, always take, and will forever take. It is sometimes hard to believe that we have nothing to offer God and that He somehow does not benefit from us. Listen to what He says: "If I were hungry, I would not tell you; For the world is Mine, and all its fullness" (Psalms 50:12). God, in His self-sufficiency, has no needs, but He says to us that *if* He had a need, He wouldn't even tell us! Why? Because anything we would use to meet that need is not ours but His to begin with. We have nothing to give God—everything is already His.

The greatest picture of God not seeking His own is Jesus Christ. God, for some reason beyond our comprehension, decided not to send us all to hell, but to give the most costly thing for our redemption. He sent His Son to live among us, clothed in humanity, and to suffer and die for us. Jesus, God's greatly loved Son, became the object of His Father's wrath. The end result? We have been adopted into God's family. We get to experience the same love the Father has for the Son. It truly was a great cost and we benefit abundantly, but the sobering truth is that even though God desires us as His children, He does not benefit from having us as His children. Because God is not seeking His own, we are the only ones that profit from our relationship with Him.

The proper response to the enormity of God's love is awe and amazement. The fact that God does not benefit from us, but that we are constantly receiving blessings from Him, should humble us. We cannot earn God's love or get on His good side. We cannot show Him that we were a good choice, because none of us were; in fact, we were all the worst possible choice—completely defiled and His sworn enemies. God is not looking for anything from us, and the truth is we have nothing to give Him if He was. We need to stop trying to earn God's love and start accepting it.

The truth that we have nothing to offer God should make us feel great, because if we don't have anything to offer Him, that means He's not looking for anything from us, which also means that when we fall short it doesn't affect Him, because He was never counting on us to do anything for Him anyway. What does that run on sentence mean for us? FREEDOM!

You are free from the performance hamster wheel that is your life, you don't need to listen to that nagging in your soul to earn your keep in the kingdom of God. You don't have to prove anything to God.

I once took a Driver's Ed class that had copious amounts of daily homework. I got very behind in the homework and I was going to fail the class if I didn't do something. So I approached the teacher and asked him, by the urgings of my mom, if I could do any extra credit work to make up for my grade. His response was like a cheese grater to my sixteen-year-old soul. He said, "If you were unable to fulfill the minimum requirements of the class, the daily homework, there's no way you will be able to do a sufficient amount of extra credit work to effect your grade." I was crushed and I failed that class.

As harsh as he was, the teacher had the right outlook when it comes to performing for God. We are incapable to do the minimum required of us from God. That's why He sent Jesus to die on our behalf. There is no extra credit we can possibly do to make up for our lack. All the good we do still gives us an "F" and no amount of work can make up for that. Besides, all the good that we do is not even our good works. They are God's works that he has prepared for us and out of His kindness allows us to partake in (see Ephesians 2:10).

If you have a performance mentality, these truths might threaten your sense of self-worth, and that should tell you something. Often, we learn that our worth and value is derived from what we do and how well we do it. You might have had parents that only showed love and approval when you performed well. Or you might have learned that you can get love and approval from teachers and peers if you are super helpful.

But some of us have an opposite reaction to earning worthiness through performance. Some of us have given up hope at earning worth through performance. We accept our worthlessness as a forgone conclusion and instead of living on the performance treadmill we never try in life. I used to suffer from this mentality. I realized I would fail no matter what I did and not trying was much easier than trying and failing, so I just never tried at anything.

It's very interesting how both the lazy and the performance mentality are driven by inner worth and value. But whichever side of the coin you're on, both types of people need to hear the same truth—value is given by God and needs to be accepted by faith.

You are valuable because God values you. And how much does He value you? Well, the value or worth of something is determined by what someone is willing to pay for it. This is clearly seen in the art community. There are no objective standards to determine the value of a piece of art. What makes a painting worth one million dollars is that someone paid a million dollars to buy it.

How much did God pay for you? He sent His Son to die for you. He looked at you and said, "I am willing to pay My Son for you." That means that to the Father, you are as valuable as Jesus. He places as much value on you as He places on His Son. Now, I don't care how good you are or how hard you work, you will never be able to add that kind of self-worth to your life.

Like most truths, this needs to be accepted by faith. Choose to believe it. Use the tools I've already shared to help it sink in. Stop listening to yourself and start talking to yourself. Tell yourself the truth until you believe it. Every morning, stand in front of your mirror, agree with God, and affirm the value He has placed on you. Lead your heart by changing your thoughts and actions regarding this truth. I've given you some great tools. Use them until the truth of your worth sinks deeply into your soul.

MAKING IT REAL

Not only does God not receive anything from us, but He is also the only one in the relationship that gives. He does all the giving and you do all the taking. But before you start feeling bad about that, realize that God would have it no other way. He gives and gives, we take and take, and it pleases Him to have it so! It brings Him great pleasure to give good things to His children—it brings God great pleasure to give you good things.

To help this truth sink in and cause your heart to overflow with thanksgiving, in the space below list fifty good things God has given you. Now, you might be tempted to go after the low hanging fruit like, "my dog" or "food". While your dog and food very well might be good things God has given you, I want to challenge you to dig deep for this exercise. What are the life changing, foundational good things God has given you?

1.	15.
2.	16.
3.	17.
4.	18.
5.	19.
6.	20.
7.	21.
8.	22.
9.	23.
10.	24.
11.	25.
12.	26.
13.	27.
14.	28.

29.   40.

30.   41.

31.   42.

32.   43.

33.   44.

34.   45.

35.   46.

36.   47.

37.   48.

38.   49.

39.   50.

LOVE IS NOT PROVOKED

GET READY

Settle yourself in a place that you can focus and without distractions. Turn off your phone if you need to. Are there any lessons that resonated with you that you'd like to spend some more time on? If you want to, you can do go back and redo an exercise or concept.

Close your eyes and take a few deep breaths. Now ask God to bless you with His presence. Just wait for a minute. You might feel a peace come over you, an inner sense of well-being, or even happiness.

Now ask God to open your heart to the truth of His love.

LOVE IS NOT PROVOKED

The next description of love is that it is "not provoked," which, in it's most basic sense, means that love does not get mad, irritated, or exasperated, nor is it embittered by injuries.[iii] Quite the opposite is true; love is slow to anger and it is not stirred to agitation. Nor does love become resentful or bitter. It does not desire to lash out or hurt those that offend it. Love pays back good for evil and blessing for harm; it is not punitive in any way.

A modern example of love not being provoked can be seen in a teenage driver who is busy flipping through the radio stations and is not paying attention to the road. As she looks up, she realizes the car in front of her is at a dead stop. Swerving to miss it she hops the curb, plows through a neighbors yard, and crashes into their garage. After receiving a call from his frightened daughter, the father shows up on scene. The daughter bursts into tears apologizing for the accident, but the father's only concern is for his daughter's safety. He is not angry at the damaged car or the neighbor's property but solely for his child. Once the bills start coming in to pay for the damages, in his mind, he would gladly pay double to keep his little princess safe. In the same way, love is not provoked by our "mistakes" but is instead concerned with our welfare.

God, in His love, is not provoked. That means that God is not mad, irritated, or exasperated with you. The reality is, that even at our absolute worst, when we deserve it the most, God has no negative feelings towards you. Why? Because all His anger and wrath—all His negative emotions towards all your failures—was poured out on the cross. He emptied Himself of His anger towards you and there is none left. His anger has been completely spent.

To say that God is mad at you is tantamount to saying that Jesus' death was not sufficient, that God is still angry about our sins, and that a further sacrifice, beyond Jesus, is still required. That is heresy and no one would readily say Jesus' sacrifice was insufficient to pay for humanities sins. But that's what some of our lives proclaim when we think God's mad about our shortcomings and we try to appease His anger somehow.

God is love. That means *you do not and cannot provoke Him*. Read that sentence again and let the profundity of it sink in. Nothing you do is sufficient to arouse His anger towards you. He is not all twisted up because of your sins. They don't freak Him out and they don't even register with Him. In Psalms 103 God says, "As far as the east is from the west," which is an infinite distance, "so far has He removed our transgressions from us." God has removed your transgressions from you and He has put an infinite distance between you and them. Here's a thought that might make your brain come oozing out of your ears: once the blood of Christ was applied to you, once you were sealed with the Spirit and adopted into His family, none of your sins ever touched you. Every sin you committed was removed from you and nailed to the cross. Now, you do have to live with the effects of your less than brilliant choices. If you have sex, you will get pregnant. That's kind of the whole purpose of sex. But the sin of premarital sex was removed from you and placed on Jesus at the cross.

But how can these things be? When Jesus died all your sins were in the future to Him. There was no distinction of time when He absorbed the Father's wrath on your behalf. God doesn't deal with your sins one at a time. He dealt with them once and for all. When you became His child, all your sins were forgiven—past, present, and future. He separated all of them from you. When you sin, God doesn't freak out and say, "Oh no, I forgot to put that one on the cross! I don't know what to do now! Hey Jesus, I might need to send you back down there. Why? Because I forgot to put all the sins on you. I know, I'm sorry, I just got distracted with the whole earthquake, and tearing the veil down the middle."

The truth is, the only one that freaks out about your sin is you. God has already permanently dealt with everything you are ever going to do. Yes, even that one sin that you are ashamed of and haven't told anyone. Even that one has been removed from you.

But wait, it gets better! Not only is God not provoked because of you; He is also not disappointed in you! It's actually impossible for God to be disappointed.

Disappointment comes from unmet expectations. For example, my wife has certain expectations regarding special occasions and gifts. Sadly, I am a horrible gift giver. Sometimes I have even been down right un-thoughtful. In the beginning of our marriage she had high expectations of me and I often fell pitifully below what she was hoping for.

One particular time was her birthday. We went to Cabo San Lucas for her birthday and I was under the impression that the trip was going to be her present. So I didn't really plan much of anything else, except for a dinner on her actual birthday. But she was expecting more, a surprise or something—it's what she would have done for me and has done for me on more than one occasion. In case you're wondering, yes, I am a little slow on the uptake from time to time. Needless to say, she was disappointed. Her birthday was kind of a flop and it was all my fault.

God on the other hand cannot ever be disappointed with you. Why? Because His expectations of you are never wrong. You act exactly the way God expects you to act, both good and bad. Nothing ever catches Him off guard; He fully knows all your faults and failures and has applied His Son's blood to all of them equally. In fact, it can be argued that God is actually blind to your failures; He does not see you in the murky light of your sins, but in the radiant light of Jesus' righteousness. The reality is that God has nothing but feelings of goodwill towards you.

The extraordinary reality that God is not mad at you reveals a foundational truth: your relationship with God is not determined by your actions, but by His actions and His alone. What that means for us is that we don't have to beat ourselves up or make ourselves suffer. Putting ourselves on "time out" reveals a misunderstanding of God's love. It shows that we think God is mad at us and that we have to be punished in order for Him to love us again, which is truly sad, especially in light of the truth that God has already punished Jesus for all our sins and His only concern is for our welfare.

There are two common reactions to our sins. The first one I already dealt with but will briefly restate it again because it's extremely important. The reaction is the, "I don't understand how God can love me when I'm such a sinner." The short answer is that you're not a sinner anymore. All your sins have been removed from you and now you stand before God with Jesus' righteousness.

That's an amazing truth but how do you believe it when you feel so much guilt and shame? Often the answer to that question is to find it in yourself to forgive yourself. And so you go on an inner journey trying to come to a place of peace over your foolish decisions. But there is a problem with that approach—you cannot forgive yourself because you didn't sin against yourself but against God.

In Psalm 51, when David was confessing and repenting for His sins regarding Bathsheeba, he made a profound statement. If you're not familiar with what David did, while one of his military commanders, Uriah, was off at war, he committed adultery with his wife, Bathsheeba. She got pregnant, so David then tried to deceive Uriah by calling him home from the war and encouraged him to go sleep with his wife. But Uriah had too much integrity to do that, after all how could he enjoy the comfort of his wife when all the men under his command couldn't do the same? So David switched plans: he gave Uriah a note for the General of the Army. The note told the general to ensure that Uriah dies in battle. Uriah delivered his own death sentence. But it gets worse. The general sent word back to David about the war with these instructions, "If David asks why so many men have died, tell him that Uriah is also dead." What does that mean? That means that a lot of innocent men had to die in order to make sure Uriah died in battle.

So David committed adultery, tried to deceive a friend, and had not only his friend killed but also a lot of other innocent men. As David confesses to God, he makes this extraordinary statement: "Against You, You only have I sinned, and did this evil in Your sight" (Psalm 51:4). You see, ultimately when we sin, it is against God. He is the one who we offend. Yes, we hurt people, but it is God's law that we have violated.

Here's an example of how absurd it is to forgive yourself. Let's say you got a ticket for running a red light. You go to court. The judge asks you how you want to plea and you respond to him, "Your honor, I have forgiven myself for running the red light." How do you think the judge would respond to you? He would laugh in your face and declare you guilty! You don't have the power to declare yourself not guilty in a court of law; only the judge can do that. In the same way, you don't have the authority, power, or ability to forgive yourself. Forgiveness is God's and God's alone to give.

So what's the answer? Simple, you need to accept God's forgiveness. Here's the great news: He already has found you not guilty. He has already forgiven you! Instead of looking inside yourself to assuage your guilt, look to God who already has freed you from the guilt of your sin. We need to be cautious of any thoughts or beliefs that put us as the starting point and that's what the whole "forgive yourself" mentality does. I don't know if you've discovered this about yourself yet, but God is the center of the universe and when we try to be, very bad things happen.

You don't need to muster up the strength to forgive yourself. You need to believe what God has done for you on the cross. Accept it by faith. You don't need to be perfect for God to love you; you have been made perfect because of His love. God's love is so powerful that it actually perfects you. It covers all your faults and shortcomings.

As a father, I've had a few moments with my babies. One time, God spoke to me about my struggles and shortcomings. Some of them I've been trying to work out for decades with off and on success. On this particular night, Aiden had woken me up for a 3 AM feeding. He had fallen asleep on my chest and I was just so in love with him, my heart was overflowing with joy and delight over my baby boy. Then, God asked me how I would feel if Aiden had struggles of his own when he grows up. "What if, like all men, he struggled with lust? What if he had substance abuse issues? Would what you're feeling for him right now change?"

My answer then and to this day is that nothing would be able to alter the profound love I have for him. My heart would hurt for him, but my love would cover whatever flaw he will grow up with. I realized something: I am not looking for anything from him; I only want to love him. And even though he will never be perfect, my love for him makes him perfect in my eyes.

God began to speak to me about my issues and struggles throughout my life. God's love is so powerful that it actually makes me perfect even though I'm not. He is not looking for me to be perfect, but to be the object of His love.

God is not looking for you to be perfect; He only desires for you to be the object of His great love, a love so powerful that it actually makes you perfect in His sight. Accept this truth by faith.

MAKING IT REAL

We dove deep this chapter and you probably need some time to process. So, take out your pen and process in the space provided below. Thank God for not being mad or disappointed at you. If that's hard, then tell Him how you'd like to believe that. Talk to God about any guilt and shame you might have. Turn those feelings over to Him, bury the dog for the last time. Talk to Him about receiving His forgiveness. Thank Him for removing all your sins from you. Thank Him for His love that makes you perfect. Confess and declare these truths by faith.

Dear Heavenly Father,

LOVE THINKS NO EVIL

GETTING READY

Settle yourself in a place where you can focus and without distractions. Turn off your phone if you need to.

Close your eyes and take a few deep breaths. Turn over to God anything that's competing for His attention. If you have persistent thoughts about things you have to do and issues going on in your life, a great strategy is to jot them down so you don't forget it and tell yourself that you'll deal with that after you're done with your time with God.

Ask God to bless you with His presence right now. Take a few minutes and meditate on how God is not mad at you and has no negative feelings towards you. Look at what you wrote down in the last chapter's exercise if you need to review.

After you've spent some time thanking Him for His great love, ask Him to bless the rest of your time and to open your heart up to the truths He has for you in this chapter.

LOVE THINKS NO EVIL

Love "thinks no evil". Literally, love does not take evil into account, it does not keep a record of wrongs, and it does not try to keep things fair. The opposite of thinking no evil is Santa Clause. Santa keeps meticulous records of how children have behaved. Those that are naughty get a lump of coal; those that are nice get presents. He keeps an extensive list of wrongs and gives good to only those that deserve it. Love is nothing like Santa. It has no list and does not balance accounts. Love is completely unfair in the very best way possible.

Because God is love, God thinks no evil and does not keep a record of wrongs. He sets His thoughts on you, not on your faults. He does not dwell on your shortcomings; He does not play them over and over in His head. He is not interested in holding your mistakes over you, nor is He waiting for you to mess up so He can point out how wretched you are. Why? Because love does not expose sin but covers it (Proverbs 10:12).

There's a great metaphor in Isaiah that tells us that God takes our wrongs and hides them behind His back (Isaiah 38:17). Now God doesn't have a back, but the image being conveyed is that God places your sins out of His sight. He puts them somewhere that He will not see or think about them. He chooses not to look at your failures or think about your mistakes!

This truth should explode in your heart! What it boils down to is that God's love influences us. We do not influence God's love. Your faults do not taint God's love for you in the slightest—He does not let your misdeeds affect the purity of His love for you, but just the opposite is true. His love is like a powerful tsunami that you cannot stand against and no amount of shortcomings can redirect.

Regardless of how wretched you may be, you are unable to stop the overwhelming flow of God's love for you. All of your faults and failures do not change how God sees you, it doesn't change God's attitude towards you, and it doesn't change how He treats you. You are unable to alter the quality or quantity of God's love towards you. But His powerful love changes you in powerful ways; it washes away every moral defect you possess.

Knowing that God thinks no evil of you and does not keep a record of your wrongs should cause you to stop bringing your past failures into your present relationship with Him. We often carry our shortcomings with us, like an albatross around our neck, unwilling to let go of things that God has already hidden behind His back. We attempt to stand against the tide of God's love, explaining to Him why we don't deserve it. And it's true; we don't deserve it because love is totally unfair towards you in the best way possible!

As amazing as that truth is, sometimes we get stuck in the guilt and shame of our sins. It's hard to even think those truths, let alone believe them. Let me tell you a little story that really helped me understand how God doesn't think evil about me. One day, a man, who was on his way to work accidently hit and killed his neighbor's dog. His neighbor was a sweet little old lady whose husband had recently died and her dog was the only thing that got her through the difficult time. The man was laden with guilt. He wondered how she would react. He feared that the loss of her dog might send her into a depression, or worse, kill her. Then he'd be responsible for not only killing her dog, but killing her too!

He gathered his courage, picked up the dog, walked up, and rang her doorbell. The little old lady came out and he burst into tears of remorse, "Please forgive me! It was an accident! I feel terrible!" The little old lady handled it better than he thought she would, but she had a favor to ask of the man. "Please help me bury my dog in the back yard. I want to keep him close to me." The man eagerly helped her bury her poor pooch.

A week later, as the man was on his way to work, he stopped at his neighbor's house. But first he grabbed a shovel out of his car. He jumped the lady's fence and dug up the dog. He brought the dog to the front door and rang the bell. When the lady opened the door, he burst into tears of remorse, "Please forgive me! It was an accident! I feel terrible!" The little old lady was a bit stunned at seeing her dog, still covered in dirt, hanging limply from the man's arms. She forgave the man again and once again asked him to help her re-bury her dog, which he did.

The following week, the man did the same thing: dug up the dog and went to the front door. When the lady opened the door he burst into tears of remorse, "Please forgive me! It was an accident! I feel terrible!" Again, the little old lady forgave him and asked for help re-re-burying her dead dog.

Every week, the man did this over and over. It got to the point that the dog was decomposing and rotting. He has to put a handkerchief around his face to be able to deal with the stench. He carried what was left of the dog to the front door. When the lady opened the door, he burst into tears of remorse, "Please forgive me! It was an accident! I feel terrible!" Exasperated, that little old lady said, "I forgave you the first time you came to me! Stop digging up my dead dog and bringing it to me asking me to forgive you for something I already have forgiven you for! Leave the dog buried!"

Sometimes we are like that with God. We feel like our failures are so horrible and we are so filled with guilt and shame that we dig them up over and over and beg God to forgive us over and over for something he has hidden behind his back and put out of His thoughts. God never asked you to dig up your sins and bring them to Him. The dog is buried. He now wants to have a relationship with you.

But the reason that some of us get caught up in self-condemnation doesn't just have to do with a misunderstanding about God and His forgiveness. It is also a practical issue with how we approach confession.

You've probably already noticed this, but God speaks to me a lot through my kids. There is one thing that every parent of small children has to deal with and that God has used to revolutionize my approach to confession, and that is dirty diapers.

I'm a father of a four-year-old and a two-year-old. There have been many diaper changes in my life and with a third on the way in June; there will be at least two more years of dirty diapers to change. Needless to say, I have had a lot of time to think about poopy diapers and I have come to the realization that sin is a lot like poop. Now for those of you with a weak stomach or for those who have not been initiated into a baptism of dirty diapers, stay with me for a little bit.

You see, sin and poop have a lot in common:
- Both are part of the "human condition".
- Poop is filled with toxins and waste that your body needs to eliminate. Sin is a type of spiritual/emotional/mental toxin that needs to be eliminated from your life.
- If you don't eliminate your poop it will kill you. You'll go into septic shock and die if you don't get it out. If you don't eliminate your sins (through the blood of Jesus), it will kill you spiritually.
- Sin and poop both have a defiling and offensive quality.

- When children are pooping in their diapers, they hide. When we sin, we are also compelled to hide.
- A poopy diaper gets in the way of a parents ability to be close to their child. When we sin, it interferes with our closeness with God.

But here's my big insight about confession. When my kids poop in their diapers, my goal is to clean them as fast as I can so I can get back to playing, snuggling, or reading to them—it's usually snuggling, sometimes I bribe them to snuggle with me and when that doesn't work, I force them to snuggle. Just for the record, even though a forced snuggle is short lived and is something akin to trying to hug a flopping fish, in this father's opinion, it's still worth the effort.

Besides eating, sleeping, and crying, pooping is one of the most common things my kids do. When they fill their drawers with chocolate pudding, I remove the offending substance, clean them up and go back to lavishing them with affection. I never hold their dirty diaper against them. I never send them on time out because they did what comes natural. My heart is to get them to a place where there is nothing that interferes with our closeness.

That's God's heart towards you and your sins. He has already paid the price for your "poopy diapers". He wants to clean you up as quickly as possible, through confession, so you can be close to him again. But sometimes we get caught up in a form of confession that actually keeps us from God instead of drawing us closer to Him. We feel ashamed of doing what comes naturally, sinning, and so we punish ourselves. We hold God at a distance until we have felt bad enough for long enough to make up for having a blow out in our diapers. Then, with timidity, we seek to get close once again. Sometimes this process takes days or even weeks depending on how bad we think our sin was.

That approach to God would be like one of my kids putting themselves on timeout because they did what comes naturally—pooped. A loving parent desires closeness with their child. God desires closeness with you. Your sins do not freak him out—He has already taken care of them. He just wants to clean you up quickly, through confession, and get back to "snuggling" with you.

So how do you let God clean you up quickly and stop punishing yourself for your sins? I'm about to share one of the most powerful tools I have ever come across. It's from *How People Grow* by Cloud and Townsend. There are two mentalities that you can use to approach confession.

The first mentality looks like this: when you sin you think to yourself that you failed. It's a total, utter failure, and the end of the world. You are the biggest loser to ever walk the face of the earth and you are hopeless, beyond help. Typically, the next thing that goes through your mind is that God is disappointed in you that you have not only failed but that you let God down. If you've got a Catholic background, you might imagine Jesus being so disappointed in you that He is crying. The next thing you experience are overwhelming feelings of guilt and shame. Usually, you just sit in that funk for a while, dumping on yourself, whipping yourself up into a nice depression. After you have felt miserable for your sin for what you deem as long enough, you then make God a promise. You tell Him, "Next time I'll try harder."

This is the mentality that lives under the Law. There's a major problem with this mentality and that is that trying harder doesn't work. The whole purpose of the Law was to convince us of that truth. We cannot, in our own effort, ever live up to God's standards. It's a mentality that says, "If I make myself feel bad, it will help me become good." I don't know where we got the idea that making someone feel bad would help them be good, but it's disastrous to us and to our relationship with God.

The second mentality lives under grace. When you sin, instead of thinking that you failed, you simply admit that you fell. Yes, you messed up, but you're not a total failure. This is not about playing down your sins, but it's also not about exaggerating them either. Regardless of how bad your sin is, it is not going to make the world come to a screeching halt. Yes, you sinned, but by God's grace, you can recover from it. Next, instead of thinking that God is disappointed with you, you recognize that God has unmerited or undeserved favor towards you. God's favor and grace does not change based on your behavior. When you are feeling the closest to God, you have as much of His favor as you do when you are smack dab in the middle of your sin. You did nothing to earn His favor and you can't do anything to un-earn it. Understanding that should cause thankfulness: thankfulness for His grace, thankfulness for His forgiveness, and thankfulness for the cross. It should cause your heart to overflow with gratitude towards God. Finally, instead of promising God you'll try harder, you will realize that you need help: help from God and help from others.

This form of confession will draw you closer to God instead of farther because it does two things. First, it takes the focus off you and puts it on God. When you do that, the second thing happens, you begin to see your failures and God in the proper perspective. They become very small and God and His grace become very, very big.

LAW MENTALITY	GRACE MENTALITY
I failed	I fell
I have disappointed God	I have God's unmerited
Feelings of guilt and shame	favor
Promise to try harder	Feelings of thankfulness
	Admit that I need help

MAKING IT REAL

It's time to bury the dead dog for the last time and put the grace-based confession to practice.

Think about anything you feel guilty or shameful about or any sins that you have recently committed. Now, take some time and confess to God using the grace mentality.

> One word of warning: this might feel very odd to confess this way especially it you're used to beating yourself up over your shortcomings. As you begin to feel positive emotions, you might even think to yourself, "Is this okay?" The answer is yes, confession was meant to draw you into a deeper experience of God and His grace and the thing that might feel weird to you is God's grace. Enjoy it! Grab a hold of it by faith—remember it is faith that pleases God.

Write down any insights or realizations that came to you while confessing with a mentality of grace. Was it challenging? Was it freeing? What were some of the things you felt? How was this different then your normal confessions to God?

LOVE DOES NOT REJOICE IN INIQUITY BUT IN THE TRUTH

GETTING READY

Settle yourself in a place that you can focus and without distractions. Turn off your phone if you need to. Are there any lessons that resonated with you that you'd like to spend some more time on? If you want to, you can go back and redo an exercise or concept.

Now, close your eyes and take a few deep breaths. Think for a moment on some of the reasons that you love God and why you're thankful for Him in your life.

Take ten deep breaths. As you inhale, think the word "Father". As you exhale, either think or softly say, "I love you because/for your…"

Next, spend some time just enjoying God and His presence.

DOES NOT REJOICE

The next description of love is that it "does not rejoice in iniquity, but rejoices in the truth". This characteristic of love has two aspects: what love abstains from and what it engages in. Specifically, this abstaining/engaging is in regards to rejoicing, which is an inner sense of happiness and satisfaction.

Love does not rejoice or derive a sense of satisfaction from wrongdoing or iniquity. In this context wrongdoing can be active (something we do), or passive (something that is done to us). When I was growing up, my mother spanked me a lot. Evidently, I was such a little troublemaker that the principal of the school she worked at, she was an elementary teacher, gave her the school's corporal punishment paddle.

On one particular occasion, one of my sisters and I were in an altercation. I was sent to my room to think about how I responded to her, because she was the instigator. She was almost always the instigator and I almost always got spanked because of it. But this time, God had finally heard my cry for justice and retribution. She was finally going to get spanked!

So, I snuck out of my room and stood by her door and gleefully listened to each slap of the paddle. I had to cover my mouth so that my mom couldn't hear me laughing as my sister began to cry. Then I snuck back into my room and rejoiced over her misfortune. Unlike love, I had rejoiced in iniquity. I had taken satisfaction in my sister's pain.

Another example is laughing at someone who falls down. If you laugh, then you have taken satisfaction in wrongdoing. If they tripped, you were pleased that they made a mistake. If they were pushed, you were pleased that someone else did wrong to them. Once I realized this, it ruined *America's Funniest Home Videos* for me. Most of the show is centered on laughing at people's mistakes. But love is not like us; it is different, it does not rejoice when wrong is done to us or by us.

Because God is love, He finds no pleasure in our mistakes nor does He view our shortcomings as an opportunity to vindicate Himself. When we see someone make a mistake, we often find personal satisfaction in telling them, "I told you so". We do this because we enjoy proving that we are right, even at other people's expense. God, however, has no need to *prove* himself right. Only the insecure attempt to prove their rightness. Sometimes we think that God gets some kind of perverse pleasure from being able to hold our mistakes over us, reminding us of how bad we have been, but God does not use our poor choices as an opportunity to "rub it in". He takes no joy in our mistakes and never says, "I told you so!"

He also finds no pleasure in our misfortunes. He is not pleased when bad things happen to us. God is not happy when we are hurting, even if we deserve it. Moreover, God actually hurts when we hurt. Isaiah 63:9 says, "In all their affliction He was afflicted". God is not a passive spectator in our life but an active participant; every injury we suffered from others, He suffered with us. Every sin committed against us was also committed against Him, and every scar we have from this life, He has one that matches it.

Psalms says that God captures and counts every tear that you have ever shed (Psalm 56:8). Psalms also says that He is near to the brokenhearted (Psalm 34:18). There is a special closeness that you can have with God in your pain. It's a closeness that you cannot have in the good times of life.

If love doesn't rejoice when bad stuff happens to us, what does love take satisfaction in? When we walk in the truth—when our experiences line up with God's desires. Another way to say that is, God derives great satisfaction and pleasure in our momentous moments—the times we walk in the truth. He is like a parent watching their child learn to take their first steps. As the child tries and falls countless times, the parent does not focus on the failures of past attempts, but on the progress the child is making. Realize that God wants to celebrate over us, not scold us. That might be a revelation for you. If it is, stop reading and talk to God about that.

God's heart can be seen in the Apostle John's heart when he wrote to His children in Christ, "I have no greater joy than to hear that my children walk in the truth" (3 John 4 NKJV). God takes great pleasure in watching His children learn to walk and take steps of faith. He focuses on our successes, not our failures.

Because God does not rejoice in iniquity, but rejoices in the truth, it should cause us to have a particular experience with Him. An experience in which we find continual encouragement from Him; one in which He does not saddle us with discouragement. If we understand God's love for us, we will find constant reassurance and refreshment. However, if we are mistaken about God's love, if we base His love for us on our experience of love in this life, we will frequently doubt our standing before Him. The question we must ask ourselves is, "Do I think that God focuses more on my failures or my successes?" Because the truth is, He wants to celebrate over you, as He spoke through His prophets, "He will rejoice over you with gladness, He will quiet you with His love, He will rejoice over you with singing." (Zephaniah 3:17 NKJV).

I've seen this truth played out in my own life. When I turned eighteen, I moved out of my mom and step-dad's house and moved into my father's house. I loved it there, partially because I was no longer around my angry step dad and also because I got to spend time with my father in a way that I had never experienced before. We had some great conversations and heart to hearts.

Two years later, my father died on Christmas day from complications with a back surgery. I was wrecked for a long time. Eventually, I got through the grieving process and the pain of the loss subsided. But I went from loving Christmas to hating it.

Every year, everything would remind me of my dad's death. For nearly five years, my Christmas tradition would consist of me spending Christmas at my father's grave. I became a Christmas Scrooge. Two decades later, when I got married, I tried really hard to pretend for my wife that I enjoyed the holiday, but inside, it would always make me sad. I disliked Christmas so much that our house was never decorated, we never played Christmas music, and I refused to get a Christmas tree.

I had created a great reason for not getting a tree. I told everybody it's a household idol. You go and, just like the pagans in the Bible, pick out a piece of wood, bring it into your home, and set it in a prominent location in the house. You then adorn your idol with silver and gold and make it beautiful. Then you begin to offer it gifts, placing them at your idols feet. Now, I didn't actually believe that, but that's how I kept a Christmas tree out of my house. The real reason, though, is because I didn't want a reminder of my pain in my house.

My wife is wonderful. She always knew that I was sad and that I was putting on a brave face for her and her family and she wouldn't require much of me, but she'd love me a little extra during that time.

Never once did God rejoice in my pain during Christmas. But His heart broke with mine. My loss became His loss. Even now, as I'm writing this, my eyes are filled with tears and God's heart is going out to me. He is comforting me in a way I could never have experienced if I had never suffered the loss of my father.

But that's not the end of this story. Four years ago, my oldest son was born. God could have allowed us to have our first baby at anytime, but He chose to have his due date on December 25, the same day my father died. Now, Aiden came three days later, but that doesn't matter to me.

My little Aiden was God's Christmas gift to me. That year he was born and every year after, Christmas was transformed for me. The sadness was gone and I began to do things I hadn't done for over twenty years. I was excited about Christmas. I had a reason to rejoice. I began to blast Christmas music in my house, in my car, and in my office. I even bought a Christmas tree! That almost made my wife pass out.

In Isaiah 61, God promises "to comfort all who mourn, to console those who mourn in Zion, to give them beauty for ashes, the oil of joy for mourning, the garment of praise for the spirit of heaviness." And that's exactly what He did for me. He took my spirit of heaviness and gave me a spirit of praise. He took my ashes and gave me something beautiful.

Don't get me wrong. I still miss my dad and from time to time, I still get sad. But at one time, Christmas held nothing but pain for me, and now there is something to celebrate. Every Christmas, I put Aiden in my lap and I tell him that he is my Christmas present and if I never got another Christmas present again it wouldn't matter, because I have him.

At one time God grieved with me, and now he rejoices with me! He takes no pleasure in your pain. He is going to take your spirit of heaviness and give you something to praise for. He is going to take away your mourning and replace it with joy. He is going to take the ashes of your life and give you something beautiful. It might not be as fast as you like. I had to wait over twenty years for it to happen for me, but it will happen. One day God will redeem even the most painful parts of your life. Just because it hasn't happened yet, don't think that it will never happen. He will fulfill His word, He will heal the pain, and He will transform it into something beautiful.

And, until then, you can rest in the understanding that God is right beside you sharing in your hurt and extending to you His comfort.

MAKING IT REAL

God is not happy about your failures or your pain. Sometimes it's hard to believe that. Sometimes it's even harder to believe that He rejoices over all the good things that happen in your life. Take out your pen and dialogue with God about that in the space provided below.

> If you have a hard time believing it, let Him know and tell Him that you'd like to believe it. If you know and believe this truth already, talk to God about how it makes you feel. Tell him about specific instances where He grieved with you and where He rejoiced with you. Spend some time thanking Him.

LOVE BEARS ALL THINGS

GETTING READY

Settle yourself in a place that you can focus and without distractions. Turn off your phone if you need to. Are there any lessons that resonated with you that you'd like to spend more time on? If you want to, you can go back and redo an exercise or review a concept.

These "Getting Ready" exercises are designed to help you practice Psalm 131:1b-2: "I don't concern myself with matters too great or too awesome for me to grasp. Instead, I have calmed and quieted myself, like a weaned child who no longer cries for its mother's milk. Yes, like a weaned child is my soul within me."

This is a Psalm of David, King of Israel that was to be sung when approaching the temple. It was designed to get you ready to enter into God's presence. It starts with, "I don't concern myself with matters to great or too awesome for me to grasp." This is about putting out of your mind thoughts, subjects, or issues that are beyond your ability to handle with ease. All that stresses you, all that concerns you, and all that weighs on you fits into this category. As you prepare to meet with God, you want to stop the mental and emotional wheels from churning about things that you have no control over. Put them out of your mind.

The second step is to "calm and quite yourself...like a child that no longer cries for milk". The idea is to have an inner calm and quiet instead. Put away the anxiety and desperate pleas for help and just be content in God's presence.

If there is a particular exercise that we have already covered that helps you do that, please feel free to switch out any one you like the most. As I shared before, the following is one of my favorites.

Close your eyes and take a few deep breaths. While still breathing, slowly and deeply read the following either out loud or to yourself.

Be still and know that I am God
Be still and know that I am
Be still and know
Be still
Be

LOVE BEARS ALL THINGS

The word "bears" carries the connotation of supporting something, like a load-bearing wall that supports the weight of a building's roof. What does love support? Literally, "all things", which reveals that its ability to bear has no limits. The idea being conveyed is that love supports a limitless load.[iv] There is nothing that love cannot support or bear.

To fully understand what this aspect of love is, it is helpful to first understand what it is not. Think of an Olympic weight lifter struggling and straining under a bending barbell loaded with weight plates. His muscles quiver and begin to fatigue because of the demands placed on them and once the lifter reaches his limit, the barbell comes crashing down. The weightlifter, no matter how strong he is, is an example of a very limited ability to bear something. There are actually examples of weightlifters trying to bear too much with catastrophic consequences—bones break, arms get pulled out of socket, ligaments tear, and muscles detach. Painful stuff happens when something that is limited tries to bear too much. But Love, unlike the weightlifter, has an infinite ability to bear, which means it does not struggle, strain, or fatigue under any load. There is never a catastrophic failure in its load bearing ability. It can handle anything, and I don't just mean anything, but anything and everything all at once.

What does that mean? It means that God's love has a limitless capacity to bear our limited loads. The foundational theological truth behind this characteristic of God's love is His infinitude. Yes, I know that word sounds like I made it up, but it's a real word and it happens to be one of my favorite attributes of God. God's infinitude means that He is infinite and without limits, which means that His love is also infinite and without limits. God's infinitude is a difficult concept for us to grasp since every aspect of our lives are measured and limited. We measure and are limited by time, by space, by gravitational pull, by endurance, and by strength. But God defies measurement and limitation because He is infinite.

Specifically, there are three attributes that contribute to His limitless capacity to bear all things. They are His infinite strength, patience, and resolve. There is no end to His strength; nothing is too heavy for Him to lift. God does not expend energy like we do. He uses His great strength and power but loses none of it when he uses it.

There is also no end to His patience. He doesn't have a short fuse or a long fuse, because he doesn't have a fuse. God has a limitless supply of patience for us and for our burdens. It is impossible to try His patience because it is inexhaustible and indefatigable (that's a great word, you should look it up). Nothing is too difficult for Him to bear.

There is also no end to His resolve. God makes up His mind and nothing changes it! Nothing is able to alter His course. Nothing is able to convince Him to go back on His word. Mount Everest will erode into a pile of sand before God's resolve can be exhausted. Nothing can dishearten Him. Nothing can convince Him to throw in the towel or give up. There is no load great enough that can even begin to tax God's ability to bear it!

Here is a great truth that needs to sink down deep into all of our souls—God is infinite and we are not. There are definite limits to every aspect of who we are and what we do. Because we are limited, we can only produce limited things. What does that mean for you? At times, your faults and failures seem to loom over you like Mount Everest, so large and glaring that you are dwarfed by them. To you, they are insurmountable obstacles that keep you from God and His love.

But no matter how egregious your faults and failures are, the truth is that they are very limited. Your sins may be as huge as a mountain, but the mountain has limits. It doesn't stretch into infinity. Even if you sinned every moment of every day of your life, even then your sin has limits. And yes, they seem massive to you, but they are like a speck of sand to a limitless God. God bears us and all our faults and He bears the whole weight of who we are and what we have done. That load is as limited as you are and a God without limits carries it.

While it is important to know God has an infinite capacity to bear a load, you must also remember that God does not do everything that He is capable of doing. God only does that which He chooses to do. What does that mean? It means that just because God has the ability to bear you and all your junk, it doesn't mean He is obligated to.

This is the most amazing aspect of God's love: not only does He have the capacity to support us, but He actually chooses bear all of who we are, at all times, and on all occasions without exception.[v] God has freely chosen to bear you! It was not only His choice, but it was also His idea! Not only is He capable, but He also wants to bear you! Yes, you read that right!

God, in His great love, has chosen to support and bear you, and you, with all your faults, are in no way burdensome to Him. He bears you easily. You do not weigh Him down, and it never enters His mind to give up on you or throw in the towel.

Knowing that God bears all things should cause a significant change in your inner and outer life with God. Because He bears your load easily and never tires of bearing it, you can stop walking on eggshells with Him. Nothing you do or don't do will be too much for Him to bear. Read that sentence again and ask God to help it sink in. You don't have to worry about making a misstep that will cause Him to give up on you. You actually don't have the ability to cause God to give up on you. You can have confidence that God is not burdened by you, but rather that He delights in you!

This is a great truth, especially if you're weighed down by the guilt of your sins. One of the most common questions I get about God's love is, "How can God love me when I'm such a sinner?" And if that's you, I want you to read the next sentence slowly and let it sink in. You are no longer a sinner; you are a saint. If you need to go back and reread the chapter on *Love Is Not Provoked*. Your sins are not an issue, because they have been removed. That was the whole point of the cross.

But sometimes the real issue is an emotional commitment to a certain view of ourselves. We can get committed to the idea that we are so messed up that we are beyond hope, after all isn't that what our past taught us. Now we have constructed an identity and a life based on those lies and we are emotionally committed to our perception of reality. We actually need to see ourselves as messed up. We need to see ourselves as beyond hope. It's how we get our needs met in life.

The startling fact is that when you are broken, you need the drama and rejection to justify your brokenness. You tend to view the world in a way that gets you what you need in order to feel justified with how you view yourself and the world. Let me give you a few examples:

If you are an angry person you need to be provoked. If you are angry you will view most of life as a provocation. Your mindset is to be on the lookout and be hyper sensitive to anything that even looks like an insult or provocation. As a result, you will tend to lash out at others on a regular basis and of course no one likes to be yelled at, so they start yelling back. Then you get what you were looking for—justification for being an angry person.

If you're anxious, you need problems in your life. If you're anxious, you see everything as a problem. And as you see problems everywhere, you begin to panic. I don't know if you've realized this yet, but when you begin to react out of fear and panic, it seldom makes things better. In fact it usually has catastrophic consequences. And when your panic produces more problems, it justifies your anxiety.

If you have a fear of rejection, you need people to reject you. You view relationships as threatening and risky, that people are dangerous and cause hurt and pain. So, you become defensive. You build barriers to keep people at a distance. You reject them before they can reject you. And let's face it; no one likes to be pushed away or held at a distance. You keep telling them to leave you alone, so what do they do? They leave you alone. And then you feel justified in your view that people are threatening because they just rejected you.

If you're a victim, you need people to take advantage of you to feel justified in that mentality. If you're critical, you need people to be wrong to feel justified in that mentality. And if you feel worthless, you need people to treat you as worthless so you can feel justified in that mentality.

When your mentality is one of brokenness, you not only look for that brokenness, you actually need others to confirm that brokenness in your life. Even though you might not like your brokenness, you need it to meet your needs.

There is a family friend of mine that has a very predictable pattern in his life. He is one of those people that are always getting themselves into trouble. His life is constantly melting down. Whenever he has a problem, the people in his life come running to his rescue. Once the disaster is under control, people begin to get back to their own lives. He gets less and less of their time and attention, so after a while, whether consciously or subconsciously, he invents another disaster that pulls people back into his life and once again he gets the best of their time and attention. Now he hates the pattern in his life, but he can't stop because he needs the drama to get his needs met.

112

MAKING IT REAL

So, here's the million-dollar question: what do you "need" in your life to fulfill your needs? If you've been struggling with something for a while, is it possible that even though you want to be free, you are ensuring you won't be free because you need it to meet your needs?

Spend some time talking to God about this by journaling in the space below. To help stimulate your time with God you can ask yourself and God some of the following questions:

Is my identity wrapped up in brokenness of some sort?

What are my needs?

How do I get my needs met?

How do I use my issue to get my needs met?

In what ways am I emotionally committed to my issues?

What are some holy and healthy ways to get my needs met?

How can I start getting my needs met in ways that don't reinforce my issues and brokenness?

One of the most helpful things for you to begin to do is to start getting your needs met in healthy and holy ways that reaffirm your identity in Christ. As you begin to learn a new way to meet your needs it will help free you from your old patterns. So, what is one thing you can begin doing today to meet your needs in a healthy and holy way?

LOVE BELIEVES ALL THINGS

GETTING READY

Settle yourself in a place that you can focus and without distractions. Turn off your phone if you need to. Are there any lessons that resonated with you that you'd like to spend some more time on? If you want to, you can go back and redo an exercise or concept.

Close your eyes and take a few deep breaths. Invite the Holy Spirit to lead you and guide you in this time. Thank God for His nearness and His presence.

Spend a few minutes waiting on the Lord. Wait for His presence to fill you from your head to your feet. You might feel a peace come over you, an inner sense of well-being, or even happiness.

Now, lift up this time to Him, ask Him to open your heart to the truths He wants to show you.

LOVE BELIEVES ALL THINGS

Love "believes all things". The word "believe" refers to trust, specifically putting trust in someone. As with the previous characteristic of love, the term, "all things", carries the connotation of the absence of limitations. So, when the Bible tells us that love believes all things it means that love has limitless trust.

This one is particularly hard to grasp, because our views of trust are very distorted. We see trust as something that is always limited. In fact, we believe that the more limited we make our trust, the wiser we are. It keeps us from being hurt. Didn't God tell us to guard our hearts? I hate to be the bearer of bad news, but God told us to guard our hearts from evil influences that would cause us to fall into sin. He never told us to guard our hearts from people. Don't believe me? Look it up: Proverbs 4:23.

We also believe that trust is something that needs to be earned, and that people need to jump through hoops in order to earn our trust. Danny Silk, author of *Keep Your Love On*, has some great insight about our modern version of trust:

> *For many people, trust means, "I need to be able to anticipate your decisions. I need to know that you would do what I would do." On one level, that's absolutely right—two people in a relationship need to be on the same page about who they are and what they are going after. But if trust hinges on my ability to anticipate your behavior, then our connection is going to be threatened. Every time you do something that I would never do, I begin to think:* I didn't anticipate that! You aren't acting like me. I would never do that to you. Did you really just bring that into our relationship? How could you do that? I can't trust you now! *This version of trust quickly turns to mistrust, which is just another word for fear— the enemy of love and connection.*[vi]

But love's version of trust is diametrically opposed to our version of trust. To love, trust is something that is freely given, not earned, and there is no limit to the trust that love will give. Because God is love, that means He has limitless trust. The question that comes next is what does

God put His trust in? Now, as crazy as it might sound, God places His trust in you.

As image bearers, He has entrusted us with His image (Genesis 1:26-27); He has entrusted us with His creation (Genesis 1:28-30); He has entrusted us with the ability to make moral decisions (Genesis 2:15-17; Deuteronomy 30:19); He has entrusted us with spouses and children (Genesis 2:18-24; Malachi 2:15); He has entrusted us with material possessions and financial resources (Matthew 25:14-28); He has entrusted believers with true riches (Luke 16:11); He has entrusted us with the gospel (1 Thessalonians 2:4); and He has entrusted some of us, as shepherds, with souls (1 Peter 5:2-3).

Push pause for a moment and reflect on what God has trusted you with. Take out your journal and write some of these things down. As you do, you'll come to realize that there is not an aspect of your life that is not touched by God's trust.

Now here is where it really starts to get crazy. Not only does God trust you, but His trust is also limitless. It can't be taxed. It can't be exhausted. His trust is indefatigable (I told you in the last chapter that was a great word. You probably haven't looked it up yet, have you? Don't feel bad, but fair warning, I might use it again.). So what does all that mean for you? You should sit down for this one... His trust in you is not dependent on you or your performance! God does not blacklist you for being untrustworthy; that is to say that even when you are untrustworthy, God does not treat you as such. He willingly extends trust to you even after you have proven that you cannot be trusted. Let that thought sink in. Your failures don't prevent God from trusting you! His trust isn't earned and it is limitless!

Your head is probably spinning right now. Either that, or you're yelling at your tablet, kindle, or computer telling me how wrong I am. That's because we have an earthly understanding of trust. Everything in us screams that that kind of trust is for morons that like to be taken advantage of. God would revoke His trust in an instant if you messed up. That might be how people treated you in the past, but that is not what the Heavenly Father is like.

God's trust is unlimited in the respect that even though you might fail in different areas of your life, you cannot break God's trust, you cannot damage it, nor can you cause it to be revoked. Why? Because His trust is based on who He is, not who you are.

To be clear, I am not saying that there will be no negative consequences to your choices in life. If you get caught committing a crime, you will go to jail. But we can't confuse negative consequences with revoked trust. Galatians 6:7 tells us that you cannot mock God. Whatever you sow, you will reap. You cannot get out of the consequences of sinful choices, but everything that God has trusted you with is still entrusted to you—His image, His creation, your freewill, your family, your finances and material possessions, and the gospel. Your choices might affect how you can use those things, but you still retain God's trust.

This aspect of God's love is extremely counter intuitive. Everything in us says that if someone violates our trust, the appropriate response is to cut them off and never trust them again. We do this because we fear loss and attempt to protect ourselves from further injury. But praise be to God that He is nothing like us. God doesn't protect Himself by limiting the trust He places in us; He is willing to trust without limit because He is not fearful of loss.

119

One of the reasons there is such a sharp contrast between God and us on this point is because of an abundance vs. scarcity paradigm. We tend to operate with a paradigm of scarcity; we don't have much and if we see the potential to loose the little that we have, we refuse to trust. Whereas, God has a paradigm of abundance; He has everything to give and nothing to lose; therefore, He extends trust even to those unworthy of it.

As we grapple with this aspect of God's love, there is one nagging question that needs to be answered—"Why?" Why does God continue to trust us when we have proven countless times that we are untrustworthy? The answer is profound: God trusts us in order to grow us. God gains nothing from trusting us; we are the only ones that benefit from being trusted. Part of the natural maturation and development from a child into a well-adjusted adult is increasing opportunities to be trusted; not trusting a child will keep them childish forever. God places His unlimited trust in us as an opportunity to experience Him and partner with Him, to be transformed into the image of His Son.

The fact that God's trust in you is for your growth and maturity should change your response to God when you prove yourself untrustworthy. Instead of beating yourself up hoping that God will see how bad you feel and maybe trust you again, you should humbly ask for forgiveness and continue walking the path to maturity—learning from your mistakes and embracing the trust God continues to place in you.

God's intention has never been to make you feel bad, but to make you more like Him, and He does that through His closeness to you. When you realize that, you begin to understand that a lot of your wallowing in self-pity and worthlessness is counter productive. If God's goal is to make you more like Him, then how does focusing on how wretched you are help accomplish that? It doesn't. Here's a crazy thought: the reason we do it is because it makes us feel better. It's a modern form of medieval penances and self-mortification practices. It assuages our guilt.

As I mentioned in the beginning of the book, I used to have a belief that when I sinned I needed to be punished in order for God to love me again and for the relationship to be restored. I desperately desired intimacy with Him again but He wouldn't punish me, which made things worse for me. I believed it was a form of rejection. It drove me to do something extreme: I made a whip and beat my back with it till I couldn't take the pain. And remember that I was slapped around by my step-dad on a regular basis, so I had a very high threshold for pain. I used to get in fights at school and laugh at people when they hit me. I had been conditioned to take a punch and when I got hit by a kid, I realized I was about to own the other person in the fight.

Once I finished whipping myself, I would feel horrible, but there was also part of me that felt comforted. The bad part was over, and now I could get back to being close with God. The truth is, a lot of us do the same thing but in different ways. We need to feel bad after we sin so we can get to the comforting part where God receives us back into His good graces.

Here is a truth that hopefully frees you the way it freed me. God's love never changes, deviates, or alters in the slightest ever. When you're a super saint that leaps over sinners in a single bound or if you're right in the middle of sinning, the quality and quantity of God's love does not change.

Have you ever played the game "Shoots and Ladders"? Or if your Canadian, like my beautiful wife—she's the best thing Canada has ever produced--you might know it by the name, "Snakes and Ladders". It's a game in which you climb up ladders, but if you land on the wrong spot, you go down a slide and have to start all over again. That's how many of us view our relationship with God. We work hard to be good and do all the right things to stay away from our pet sins. As we do, we feel like we're climbing the ladder, getting closer to God, and experiencing more of Him. But when we sin, BOOM! We're knocked off the ladder and have to start all over again. We have lost our closeness to God. We have lost everything!

But our walk with God is not like a game of shoots and ladders. It's only a game of ladders, but it's not your efforts or goodness that gets you up the ladder. It's God who does that. It's His presence in your life. When we misstep and sin, we don't have to start all over. We get to start exactly where we left off, at the same level of intimacy and the same level of closeness.

Brother Lawrence, a sixteenth century French monk, understood all of this with an elegantly simplistic clarity. His view was that we tended to park our sins between us and God, keeping God at a distance. But if the real goal in life is to experience God and let His presence transform us, then you need to just stop doing that. This is how Brother Lawrence would confess: "This is what I'll always naturally do if I'm left on my own, Lord."[vii] Then he would begin to practice and experience God's presence once again.

It really is as simple as that if you choose to, in faith, believe God at His word. His intention has never been to make you feel bad, but to make you more like Him, and

He does that through His closeness to you. Choose to embrace that truth instead of the one that requires you to suffer before you can be close to Him again—believe it by faith.

MAKING IT REAL

God has limitless trust in you and your shortcomings don't deter His trust. He trusts you not because He gets anything out of the deal, but because you get something incredible out of it: you get to experience and partner with God and be conformed into His image.

All of us have failed in many ways. Sometimes our failures can gnaw at us and create distance between God and us. I want you to try and reframe your mistakes. Take out your journal and write down one or two of you major or most recent mistakes. God trusted you with those opportunities to grow you and even if you failed, you can still grow.

Take some time and prayerfully consider any valuable lessons that you learned about yourself or God through your experience. Remember to keep these positive.

Consider how you have or how you can grow through the experience.

Take some time and thank God for His trust in you. Thank Him for continuing to trust you even after you messed up.

Now, spend some time pressing into God's presence. Choose your favorite "Getting Ready" exercise or anything else you find helpful to focus on God's nearness.

LOVE HOPES ALL THINGS

GETTING READY

Settle yourself in a place where you can focus and without distractions. Turn off your phone if you need to. Are there any lessons that resonated with you that you'd like to spend some more time on? If you want to, you can go back and redo an exercise or review a concept.

Now, close your eyes and take a few deep breaths. Think for a moment on some of the reasons that you love God and why you're thankful for Him in your life.

Take ten deep breaths. As you inhale think the word "Father". As you exhale, either think or softly say, "I love you because/for your…"

Next, spend some time simply enjoying God and His presence.

LOVE HOPES ALL THINGS

The next attribute of love is that it "hopes all things". Hope is a specific attitude about the future, one of looking forward with confidence, to that which is good and beneficial.[viii] Simply stated, it is an eager expectation of good. Hope is like someone who has spent the night outside freezing, eagerly expecting the sun to rise to bring them warmth. It is important to note that hope is different than wishful thinking. The main difference is that hope is filled with certitude of what is hoped for (e.g. the person waiting for the sun to rise does not question the certainty of the event). In contrast, wishful thinking has no such confidence; it is an empty dream with little or no chance of becoming a reality. So not only does love have an eager expectation of good, but also that expectation is founded in reality; there is certainty that the good that is expected will come to pass. As in the previous two aspects of love, the term "all things" denotes the absence of limits. Literally, love is not limited to the good that it eagerly expects.

Because God is love, the good that God eagerly expects is not limited by anything. The question of course becomes, "What is the good that God confidently looks forward to?" The answer is you. God is eagerly looking forward to you! But not the current you. No, the you that God eagerly expects is the transformed you, the you that is free from sin, the you that is fully formed into the image of Jesus, the you that can experience Him as He originally designed you to be. The good that God is hopeful of is you standing in His presence, basking in His love for all eternity. And God is confident that all that will happen— it's a forgone conclusion to Him.

Hope is founded on confidence. If not, it is only wishful thinking. The confidence of God's hope is Himself. He has made an oath, swearing by Himself that He would bring immeasurable good to you, or more accurately, bring you to the immeasurable good of Himself. Hebrews 6:17-19 (NLT) says, "God also bound himself with an oath, so that those who received the promise could be perfectly sure that he would never change his mind. So God has given both his promise and his oath. These two things are unchangeable because it is impossible for God to lie. Therefore, we who have fled to him for refuge can have great confidence as we hold to the hope that lies before us. This hope is a strong and trustworthy anchor for our souls. It leads us through the curtain into God's inner sanctuary." God's promises to us are like an anchor for our souls—it keeps us safe and secure through the storms of life.

God's Hope is based on His confidence and His confidence is based in His omniscience, omnipotence, and sovereignty. Because God is omniscient (all-knowing), He already knows for a fact that we are transformable. How does He know that? Because He knows the beginning from the end. In the same moment that God said, "Let there be…" He also knew you and everything about your life. He knew you at your birth. He knew you when you accepted Jesus as your Savior. He'll know you at your deathbed. He knows you in heaven worshiping Him for eternity.

If you really want your brain to start melting out of your ears, in a very real sense, from God's perspective, you are already in heaven, in glory, and in perfect conformity to Jesus. He doesn't make a promise like we do. When we make promises, we aren't 100% sure that we can do what we say we will. Sometimes things come up. Our promises are more like stated intentions. "I intend to do 'X' for you tomorrow." But, when God makes a promise, its not because He's hoping things will work out; when He makes a promise it's because He has already fulfilled it. He looks into our future and declares to us what He has already done.

His confidence is not based on His omniscience alone, but also His omnipotence. Omnipotence means all power. Literally, God has all power. Now, follow my thought here. Logically, if God has ALL power, how much power does anyone else have? Yes, the correct answer is none. Any power that anyone or anything exercises here on earth, or in heaven for that matter, is God's power that He is allowing them to borrow. God has all power and ability. There is nothing that is too difficult for Him. Jeremiah 32:17 says, "Ah, Lord God! Behold, You have made the heavens and the earth by Your great power and outstretched arm. There is nothing too hard for You." By God's omnipotent power, He spoke the entire universe into existence in six days and He did it all without expending any of His power. He had as much power after He was done creating as He did before He created. If God can create the entire universe without draining any of His power He has more than enough power to transform you and me!

God's confidence that He can transform you is not only based on His omniscience and His omnipotence, but also His sovereignty. God's sovereignty means that He has supreme authority. He is the ruler of all. Whatever He decrees happens. There is literally no other option but to obey; all of creation, down to the molecules in your body and the sofa you're sitting on right now, is compelled to conform to God's sovereign decrees. There's this idea that there will be an epic battle between good and evil when Jesus comes back. No, there will not. Revelation tells us that Jesus shows up and everybody dies. The army that comes with Him isn't there to fight, but to watch. God has decreed that you be transformed into the image of His Son. What that means for you is that you *will be* transformed. You do not have the power to resist God. No matter how messed up you are or how stuck in your sins you may seem, you are incapable of resisting God. As sure as the sun will rise tomorrow, you will be transformed, warmed in the light of God's love.

Because God's hope cannot be limited, that means that ultimately you cannot change what God is eagerly expecting. Regardless of how much of a failure we might be, because God is hopeful towards us that He will never give up on us. Even at your lowest point, when you feel more like a child of darkness than of light, God does not and will never think of you as a lost cause. He will never think of you as hopeless or beyond His ability to help. He will never doubt, question, or stray from the promise He made to you. God's hope is based on who He is and what He is capable of, not on you and what you did or didn't do.

The fact that God hopes is what allows us to have hope. The potential of transformation is the essence of hope,[ix] and because He is confident that He can transform us, we gain the strength to keep fighting the good fight. As the author of Hebrews wrote, "This hope we have as an anchor of the soul, both sure and steadfast..." (Hebrews 6:19). God's eager expectation is the anchor permanently fixed to our soul that allows us to ride out the storms of life. You *will* arrive at your final destination. You *will* be perfected. That is something you can eagerly expect with absolute certainty.

This is a powerful truth that needs to sink deep down to where we really live. And this amazing transformation that is taking place in our lives all started with God's forgiveness. Forgiveness is a powerful thing that has the ability to radically transform us, and I'm not just talking about God's forgiveness of us, but about our forgiveness of others.

I have already told you a little bit about my childhood, how my step-dad was physically and verbally abusive. I used to hate him. At one time I even planned on killing him, but the love I had for my mom stopped me. Once I moved out of his house, stopped talking to him, and went to live with my father, God began to speak to me about forgiveness. Still, I couldn't let go of the injustice that I had suffered through my step-dad.

130

Over the years, I began to realize that my unforgiveness towards him was eating me up inside. My anger for him was actually perpetuating my brokenness and victim mindset. It was keeping me from inner healing. What I realized was that he hurt me in the past, but I kept hurting myself everyday after that through my unforgiveness.

Eventually, I realized that my healing was more important than a sense of vindication and justice, which was really just a desire for revenge. I had to free my step-dad from the debt I was holding over him, not for his sake, but for mine. As I began to forgive, something amazing happened. My relationship with God began to grow to a whole new level. I discovered something important: our relationship with God is often limited by our relationships with others. What I mean by that is that if there is bitterness or unforgiveness in your heart towards someone, then you also bring those things into your relationship with God. After all, those things are in your heart and God wants love to be in your heart. The apostle John tells us that you cannot say that you love God if you hate your brother (1 John 4:20).

If you're looking for a breakthrough with your relationship with God, it may be that you need a breakthrough in a relationship with someone else first; you may need to get rid of your bitterness and unforgiveness. Here are a few truths that may help you. First, forgiving someone is not approving of what they did. What they did was wrong and you are not saying that it was okay. You are only saying, "I will no longer harbor hate in my heart." Those are two very different things. God will deal with them for what they have done and believe me; He will do a much better job than you will. Second, just because you forgive someone, it doesn't mean everything will be candy canes and lollipops. The pain won't magically go away. Instead, what forgiveness does is it keeps the pain in the past and not in your present.

The topic of forgiveness is huge and has a big impact on every aspect of your life. You might have a lot of questions about how to walk through forgiveness in your life and how to deal with someone that keeps hurting you. Unfortunately, this is not a book on forgiveness and I can't go into all of those details, but the good news is that there are a lot of great books out there. In fact, I am almost done with a book I have been working on since God first called me to forgive my step-dad.

Also, I am almost done with a book I have been working on since God first called me to forgive my step-dad. It's a result of the journey that God took me on to not only forgive my step dad, but to love him too. I'm always asked about what my relationship with him looks like now. We have a good relationship. I love and care for him. It is a testament to God's ability to restore—His power knows no limits. If you want to hear more about that journey, or want to keep up to date on other projects I'm producing, you can sign up by visiting **www.scottwessell.com/updates/**

MAKING IT REAL

"God will transform you" is a forgone conclusion. But God's attitude is that He is eagerly awaiting you in heaven. Remember that feeling you had as a child on Christmas morning? You were excited and filled with anticipation about the amazing things that Santa left for you under the tree? God feels something similar towards your arrival and glorification in heaven.

Or an even better metaphor is when you're about to get married. The doors to the church are about to open up and you are about to see your soul mate for the first time on your wedding day. I remember when I was standing at the altar, I was so eager to see my beautiful bride adorned head to foot in gorgeousness. Even though it was just a few moments, it felt like I was staring at the closed doors for an eternity.

Every second that passed was excruciating—everything in me wanted to see her and be with her. When the doors opened, the sun was lighting up all the sparkles on her dress—she was stunning. At that moment, everything else disappeared. She was all there was. I don't even remember the ceremony because I was lost in not only her beauty, but also the moment, the day I had been waiting for over two years to happen. That's closer to how God feels about you.

Take a moment to process that. Close your eyes and think back to a particularly fond Christmas or another event where you were filled with excitement and anticipation. Take a few moments and relive that memory. What were you thinking? What were you feeling? Did you want that moment to stop? If so, why? If not, why?

Just sit in that place for a little bit, enjoy those memories and notice the feelings that you're experiencing.

Now, take a moment and imagine God feeling similar about you. How does it make you feel thinking that God can't wait to see you? What thoughts go through your head? Are your feelings and thoughts in line with how God feels about you? If not, why? What do you want to say to God right now?

Take out your pen and in the space below talk to Him about His love that eagerly awaits you.

LOVE ENDURES ALL THINGS

GETTING READY

Settle yourself in a place that you can focus and without distractions. Turn off your phone if you need to. Are there any lessons that resonated with you that you'd like to spend some more time on? If you want to you can go back and re-due an exercise or concept.

For this exercise, take out your journal and review what you talked to God about from the last chapter, regarding how He eagerly awaits you.

Close your eyes and take a few deep breaths. Invite God into this time. Now, take a few minutes and meditate on aspects of your journal entry that really stand out to you.

After you're done, ask God to speak to you in this time and open your heart to the truth of His love.

LOVE ENDURES ALL THINGS

This is the fourth "all things" statement that Paul makes and once again the term "all things" carries the connotation of limitless. The concept of endure is best summed up by the word persevere. The idea is that Love perseveres and remains steadfast and unmovable in the face of difficulties, obstacles, or discouragement. When Paul says that love endures all things, not only does he have in mind that love is unmovable in difficulty but also

135

that it does so without impairment—love is not adversely affected by the things it endures.

The opposite of this characteristic can be seen in erosion. If you have ever had the chance of seeing the Grand Canyon you will be amazed that such a massive hole in the ground is caused by the small, serpentine ribbon called the Colorado River. Over time the movement of water cut through stone and created the spectacular canyons. Love however, does not slowly get worn down or erode. The opposite is true; love has limitless endurance and endless perseverance.

Because God is love, He has limitless endurance and endless perseverance. What does God endure? The answer to that question is found in the first aspect of love, which is that it suffers long. What is it that God suffers and endures? Us—our sinful nature that seeks self-gratification, self-preservation, and self-exaltation over righteousness and God's kingdom. The truth of the matter is that we do not benefit God in any way—there is no personal profit to Him. Our relationship with God only costs Him. In Isaiah 64:6 God calls our best efforts "bloody rags". The fact is that God endures every aspect of us, even when we are on our best behavior. Even though there is much about us that God endures, His endurance is limitless, which makes it impossible for God to be exhausted or worn down by us.

God's ability to endure is influenced by His unlimited, omnipotent power. That means that God is able to use all His power for all of time without losing any of that power. Or to say it another way, when God uses His power it does not tax Him at all or drain His power in any way. God is not like the Grand Canyon, no agent exists that can exert enough force for enough time to cause erosion with Him. Indeed, He stands immutable and unchanged forever. The reality is that you cannot chip away at God. Regardless of how wretched you might be, you cannot cause God to cease enduring you.

Tragically, sometimes we buy into the fallacious notion that we are too messed up, too much of a hassle, or too insignificant for God. But thinking of ourselves in that light, that we're too much for God to endure, is blasphemous. It is tantamount to saying "I am more powerful than God". This kind of mindset is a result of thinking too much of ourselves and too little of God. The correct perspective is that on our best day we cannot stop the sun from rising and we are even more incapable of stopping God from enduring. The reason we are not too much for God to endure is that enduring takes nothing from God—He has always been and will always be the same regardless of us.

Not only does God endure us, He also does so willingly. That's often the truth we really need to let sink in deep. We need to remember that we were not forced on God, He choose us knowing He would endure us, and He did so with delight! Knowing this should cause us to stop resisting God's love. You cannot do anything to change His love and you can't do anything to get Him to stop loving you. We need to fully embrace our place, we are objects of God's love, and we need to embrace being loved by Him. Some of us have spent too much time and energy trying to convince God that we are unlovable. We need to submit to the inevitable—God's love is the most powerful force in our lives and eventually it will over power every aspect of us.

Because God has a limitless ability to endure and persevere it also means that God never has to take a break from you. I try hard to be a great dad, but I am far from perfect (please don't tell my wife, I think I still have her fooled) and sometimes my kids drive me to the edge. I don't know what it is about them, but sometimes they seem like hyenas. They identify which parent is weak or sick, and then they single them out, cutting them off from the other. Then they attack, not like a lion that takes down it's prey with one vicious attack, but with small nips and bites until their prey weakens and succumbs to the inevitable.

All jokes aside, they have a sixth sense to know when I'm tired and don't have a reserve of patience. Then they come and start pushing my buttons. Doing things that they know I don't like. And I try very hard to give them the attention they are seeking from me, but sometimes I get to the point that I need a break. So, if I still have a semblance of self-control I'll tap out and have my wonderful wife run interference while I take a break. But sometimes, when I have been pushed beyond my limits everyone goes on time out.

God is nothing like me. He never needs to take a break from you, He never needs to cool off because you've been pushing His buttons, and He never puts you on time out. In fact the opposite is true, God wants to spend as much time with you as possible. He wants to lavish you with His attention. It brings Him great joy to interact with you even when you're having a bad day—remember your bad moods don't cause God to have a bad mood.

Let me tell you a story to help give you picture of how much God wants to interact with you. When Aiden, my first son, was born it was glorious. They took him and gave him to my wife for a little bit to bond. Then they needed to do hospital stuff, weigh him, measure him, and check his vitals. I followed him to the little table where they did all that. He was freaking out a little bit with all the bright lights and the dramatic change in his environment. I leaned over and began to speak to him. The second he heard my voice he stopped crying and turned his head towards me and looked at me intently. The nurse saw how he responded to me and said, "He recognizes daddy's voice." When I heard that and recognized the truth of it, a wave of emotion came over me and I almost—ALMOST—started to cry. My heart was so overjoyed to think that he knew and could respond to my voice. That was the moment he stole my heart.

Similarly, God desires to interact with you and spend time with you. He leans over you and speaks softly and lovingly to you and when you respond to Him, His heart melts (Zeph 3:17). Even after you mess up, God's desire is to, as quickly as possible, go back to being close to you.

The question I'm asked frequently is, "I know that God wants to spend time with me but how do I make Him more real to me, how do I go from understanding the thought to actually experiencing Him?" My answer is always, "By practicing the presence of God" which, by the way, is another way of saying pray without ceasing (1 Thes 5:17).

How do you practice the presence of God? Well, I've been teaching you how to do that through the getting ready exercises but it really is a simple process. You simply push pause on whatever you're doing, take a moment and lift your heart up to the Lord—tell Him you love Him, thank Him for His presence, ask Him to be with you, etc. What I usually do is I'll take a deep breath in and as I do I will think the word "Daddy" or "Abba" and as I exhale I will think or say, "I love you". I do this when I'm driving, when I'm working on the computer, when I'm watching cartoons with the kids, when I'm cooking, and even when I'm preaching. And God always responds with a sense of His presence and pleasure. There's a peace that settles over me. It's usually accompanied with a smile and sometimes when His presence is strong a little laugh of amusement.

Practicing God's presence is a simple way to revolutionize your daily experience of God. When you do it, you realize that God's heart is to connect with you and every time you lift your heart up to Him He responds to you with great joy.

MAKING IT REAL

Take a moment and try it right now, lift your heart up to Him. If you're having a blockage, try to accept His presence by faith, because the truth is that His Spirit lives in you and His presence is always with you.

Here are a couple of practical tips that you can employ to remember to practice God's presence on a regular basis.

Use your technology to help draw you closer to God.

- Set up a reminder on your phone. I have a reminder that comes up every time I get out of my car. It's a verse that I'm meditating on. Every time I see the reminder, I open it up and talk to God about the verse.
- Set an alarm on your phone or watch. I have an Apple Watch and every morning the alarm is set to go off at a certain time, usually after my morning meetings. When the alarm goes off I hit snooze then I take a second and practice God's presence. Then 9 minuets later (that's the default snooze for Apple's gadgets) I hit snooze again and lift up my heart to God again. I do this throughout the day. To be honest, I do this most days but

140

not every single day, but the days that I do are usually much more enjoyable for me.

- Set up a countdown timer on your computer. When I was going to seminary and working on the computer for hours and hours on end, I set up a Google countdown timer that would run on a side banner on my screen (this is before I saw the light and switched to Mac). Every 30 minutes it would go off. I would give my body a break but more importantly I would give my spirit a break by reconnecting to God.

Set up other reminders

- I always get questions from those who don't own smart phones how they can apply similar strategies. Well, back in the day when I had a remedial phone I learned to write the letter "P" on the back of my hand. The "P" stands for Presence and it is a visual reminder for me to turn my heart towards God. I still do this and it actually is my favorite reminder. Unlike the phone, which is intrusive at times, the "P" on my hand seems to catch my eye when I need to see it the most and reminds me to re-center myself in God's presence.

- You can also set up notes for yourself. In your car, on your mirror, at your desk, etc. I recently visited someone's house and saw something I really liked. The person had taken dry erase marker and wrote on all of her mirrors and even her windows. Everywhere you looked in the house was an inspirational reminder. I haven't tried this yet because I am unsure if my wife will be okay if a tag our entire house and I might be teaching the kids something I don't want them to learn, that it's okay to write on the house with markers.

Take some time right now and think of and decide on three different ways you can remind yourself to practice God's presence throughout your day. Now, set up those reminders up before you do anything else.

LOVE NEVER FAILS

GETTING READY

Settle yourself in a place where you can focus and without distractions. Turn off your phone if you need to. Are there any lessons that resonated with you that you'd like to spend some more time on? If you want to, you can go back and redo an exercise or review a concept.

Close your eyes and take a few deep breaths. While still breathing, slowly and deeply read the following either out loud or to yourself.

Be still and know that I am God
Be still and know that I am
Be still and know
Be still
Be

Now, take a few moments and enjoy God's presence. Lift your heart up to Him. Invite Him to speak to you in this time and to open your heart to the truth of His love.

LOVE NEVER FAILS

The final characteristic of love is that it "never fails". The word "fails" means to be without effect, to be in vain.[x] So, the idea being conveyed is that love is never without result, it always produces a change, and it is completely efficacious. One recent example of something that does fail, or does not have an effect, is government economic stimulus spending. During this country's economic recession, the government spent trillions of dollars to stimulate the economy and was unsuccessful. Love on the other hand, is a catalyst that always stimulates the object of its affection. Or to put it another way, love always changes the one that is being loved.

Because God is love, God never fails. He always produces a result, He is always stimulating change, and He is never without effect. The specific context here is the effect that God's love has on us. Because He is the uncreated Creator, the unmoved mover, the one who effects all things and is affected by nothing and because we are the object of His affection, we will be moved, affected, and changed. The eternal truth, as a believer, is that it is impossible to be loved by God and remain the same.

It is important to note that even though you have the ability to exercise your will, ultimately you cannot thwart God's love. Some of us have made self-destruction an art form; we are masters of undermining ourselves and expunging any good from our lives. The amazing news is that regardless of how good we are at shooting ourselves in the foot, we cannot stop the effect of God's love on us. Now, it is possible to limit your experience of God's love and it's even possible to slow down the effect of God's love in your life, but the one thing you can never do is to stop it altogether. God's love will have its way with you. Stop and let that thought sink in.

If that is true, the question then becomes, "What is the effect that love is/will have on me?" To name just a few, one effect of God's love is that we have been drawn to Him. He declares, "I drew them with gentle cords, with bands of love…" (Hosea 11:4 NKJV). Because we are fallen, we would not have come to God without His love drawing us to Him.

Another effect of God's love on us is that it leads us to repentance (Romans 2:4). Without God's loving-kindness, we would remain unapologetically proud and rebellious. It is only because of His love that we came to the place where we surrendered our right to ourselves. If it were not for His love we would still be stuck in our sin.

One of the greatest effects of God's love is our adoption into His family. "See what great love the Father has lavished on us, that we should be called children of God! And that is what we are!" (1 John 3:1 NIV). God lavished (excessively displayed) on you His great, extraordinary, otherworldly love by adopting you into His family. He not only saved you from hell, He not only sealed you with His Spirit, He is not only preparing a place for you, but He has invited you permanently into His family. The Heavenly Father has included you into the same quality of a relationship that He has with His Son, Jesus Christ. He has given you the same acceptance that He has for His Son! He has given you the same intimacy that He has with His Son! He has given you the same affection that He has for His Son! There is nothing that the Father feels for the Son that He does not feel for you! God's love has changed you into His child.

Another important effect of God's love for us is that we are capable of real love. "We love because He first loved us." (1 John 4:19). Without God's effectual love, you could not love God, and your love for others would be selfish and twisted without it. But because He loves you, you now know what love is and can reflect it back to Him and to those around you.

Knowing what effects God's love has caused in your life should cause you to be eager to experience and express more of His love. You experience His love by embracing your position as His child. Instead of holding your Father at arms distance, you should take every opportunity to explore what being His child means. And you express His love by loving others in the same manner that He has loved you.

Which brings me to my final thought before we close this book. There are two components to understanding God's love that really must be in place in order to fully understand and experience it. The components are the two types of relationships that we were created to experience. Looking at God's original design before sin entered the world, the first type of relationship we were made for is a vertical one. You need a solid connection to God and thankfully through the blood of Jesus, we can be restored to the kind of relationship we were created for.

The second type of relationship you were created for is seen in God's comment about Adam after he created him. Every day, after God created something, He saw that "it was good." But after He saw Adam, God said, "It is not good for the man to be alone." I always like to ask the question, "In what way was Adam alone?" He had what most of us long and dream for—a perfect relationship with God that is unbroken by sin. But God saw Adam, who had a perfect relationship with Him, and in effect said, "Adam needs someone besides me." Yes, you were created to need God, but you were also created to need relationships with others.

A major problem in western Christianity today is an individualistic approach to spirituality. We often focus on the vertical relationship with God and ignore the horizontal relationships that God created us to have. Too often we get the mentality that we can have bad relationships in our lives but have a great relationship with God. Unfortunately, the Bible disagrees. 1 John tells us that how well you know God is revealed in your relationships, and not just the really good ones.

You don't believe me? Look at these verses: "Beloved, let us love one another, for love is of God; and everyone who loves is born of God and knows God. He who does not love does not know God, for God is love" 1 John 4:7-8. Your understanding of God is revealed in your love for others.

"We know that we have passed from death to life, because we love the brethren. He who does not love his brother abides in death. Whoever hates his brother is a murderer, and you know that no murderer has eternal life abiding in him." 1 John 3:14-15. If you have a bad relationship with someone that is not characterized by love, than you are guilty of murder.

"If someone says, 'I love God,' and hates his brother, he is a liar; for he who does not love his brother whom he has seen, how can he love God whom he has not seen?" 1 John 4:20. This one really puts the nail in the coffin. You are self-deceived, a liar, if you think you can love God and have bad relationships with others. By bad relationships, I mean ones in which love is not present. And just to answer the age-old question, "Can you love someone without liking them?" The answer is no. How would you feel if God loved you without liking you? How about your marriage? Would you like your spouse to love you but not like you? Your best friend?

The main principle to understand is that your vertical and horizontal relationships are interrelated. If you've got bad relationships with others it will affect your relationship with God. But the good news is that it also works the opposite direction. When you begin to have better relationships with others, it improves your relationship with God. This is an important principle to understand when wanting to grow in your understanding and experience of God's love.

Your ability to love and be loved by others actually helps you understand God's love. For example, if you struggle with the concept of grace with God, you will also struggle in the same area with others, probably not giving grace, but receiving it from others. So, if you begin to allow others to show you grace and stop trying to be strong, you will also begin to accept God's grace.

So, what do you do with all this information? You examine what areas or aspects of God and His love you struggle with and chances are that you have those same issues in your other relationships. So, you attack the issue from both sides. Practice putting truth into your heart and believe it by faith, basically what I have been trying to teach you this entire book, but also begin to engage people differently too. If your issue is being strong, then ask others for help. If your issue is trust, then take baby steps and trust some people around you.

Bottom line, if you really want a breakthrough with God and experiencing His love, than you also need to work on your relationships here on earth as well.

MAKING IT REAL
Let's take some time and practice what we just talked about. Take out your pen and spend some time asking God to help examine your heart by answering the following questions.

What are your core issues with God and His love?

How do those issues with God also play out in your other relationships? Be as specific as possible.

What can you do in those relationships that would help address your issues? Be as specific as possible.

What three relationships do your issue(s) come out the most?

How do they come out in each of those three
relationships?

What one thing can you do in each relationship that will be
a positive step forward in overcoming your issue(s)? Be
highly specific.

Now that you have identified what you can do, now comes
the hard part. Write down exactly when and how you are
going to do those things.

Take out your phone. Call or text someone what
you're going to do and when you're going to do it by and
ask them to follow up with you to keep you accountable.

> Keep coming back to this exercise every week or so
> until you begin to do this naturally.

Burnout Proof Your Life In 3 Days At ReIgnite Retreat!

Let's face it... it's tough out there. And things seem to only be getting worse.

Stress, anxiety, busyness, and depression seem to creep into our daily lives and they reek havoc.

As a result, there's a **lack of peace, spiritual numbness, and feelings of guilt for not spending more time with God**. But who has the time for a quiet time when **life is so filled with distractions and struggles**?

You're Not Alone

The good news is that you're not alone and it's not your fault. You're not a failure... you just haven't been set up for success.

The truth is there are ways to make your time with God bland and unfulfilling and there are ways to make your time with God rich and deeply fulfilling. Unfortunately, **most of what we have been told to do leads to mediocre time with God**.

Let's be honest... if you have to decide between having an okay time with God or fixing a major stressor in your life which one will you choose? If you're anything like me you'll choose to try and fix the stressor over having a unfulfilling time with God.

What I Found Shocked Me!

As I said, the problem isn't you; it's your approach to spending time with God that is failing you. But, the good news is that **there is a better way and I want to share it with you**.

As a young believer, people would tell me to read my bible, spend time with God, and reflect on scripture. I'd always ask for guidance on what that actually looked like but I was never satisfied with the answer of, "**Just spend time with God and you'll figure it out**."

But that kind of advice leads to lackluster time with God; blindly groping in the dark trying to figure out how to make a connection to God. I soon realized that those who were giving me that advice were only telling me what they were told and they too were not satisfied with their time with God… it was a perpetuating cycle.

Fed up with all the unhelpful advice I was getting, I decided to dig deeper and **I was shocked at what I found!** There was a wealth of tips, techniques, and strategies to having powerful time with God that had been **"lost" to modern Christians**. For some reason, about a hundred years ago giving practical tools to connect with God fell out of vogue and **the rest of us have been suffering ever since!**

Once I started applying some of the "forgotten" techniques **there was a radical shift in my time with God.** It became so rich and rewarding that skipping it became impossible. I began to long for more time with God; I began thinking about what I could cut out of my schedule to sneak in some more daily time with him.

Would you like to have such amazing time with God that skipping it stops being an option for you?

Image how your day-to-day life would change if your experience of God were that profound?

ReIgnite Your Relationship With God

Since I made the discovery of the "lost" art of quiet time people started noticing a change in me. As a result, they began to ask what I was doing differently.

As they began to apply the simple but powerful techniques their relationship with God was radically transformed too!

Several of the people who I've shared with have been asking me to **make these "secrets" more readily available** to anyone who wants a better daily experience of God.

After some prayer and gentle urging by my friends, I was convinced that **I couldn't keep these techniques to myself anymore.** It's too important not make them available to whoever wants to use them.

So, **I decided to teach all my "secrets" at a 3-day retreat called ReIgnite!**

The ReIgnite retreat will be a time of **pushing pause on the busyness of life, connecting with God powerfully, and learning how to make a mountain top experience an every day experience for you**.

If you'd like to **say no to the stress and busyness of life** that causes burn out and **revolutionize your experience of God… join me at ReIgnite!**

You can sign up for the waiting list by visiting: **www.i195.org/reignite**

Our next ReIgnite will be this winter.

But, as fair **warning… we're keeping these retreats small** and intimate in order for you to get personalized time with me and my team.

That means there is **limited number of spots available**. Once they fill up, you'll have to wait another 6 months for the next ReIgnite! Retreat.

So, **get your name on the list today so you don't miss this winter's ReIgnite!**

Visit: **www.i195.org/reignite**

ABOUT THE AUTHOR

Scott Wessell is the Director of IMPACT195 School of Ministry and a Pastor at the Rock Church San Diego. For the last decade he has been discipling and raising up the next generation of leaders within the church. He is married to Dr. Dina Wessell and together they have two boys and are pregnant with a little girl that is due in June.

FOLLOW ME:

Facebook: facebook.com/PastorScottWessell
Twitter: twitter.com/ScottWessell
Blog: ScottWessell.com

Please Leave A Review

Word-of-mouth is crucial for any author to succeed. If you enjoyed the book, please consider leaving a review at Amazon. Even if it were only a line or two... it would be a huge help.

NOTES

[i] Matthew Henry, Matthew Henry's Commentary on the Whole Bible : Complete and Unabridged in One Volume (Peabody: Hendrickson, 1996), 1 Co 13:4–7.

[ii] Matthew Henry, *Matthew Henry's Commentary on the Whole Bible : Complete and Unabridged in One Volume* (Peabody: Hendrickson, 1996), 1 Co 13:4–7.

[iii] Anthony C. Thiselton, *The First Epistle to the Corinthians : A Commentary on the Greek Text* (Grand Rapids, Mich.: W.B. Eerdmans, 2000), 1052.

[iv] Anthony C. Thiselton, *The First Epistle to the Corinthians : A Commentary on the Greek Text* (Grand Rapids, Mich.: W.B. Eerdmans, 2000), 1058.

[v] Robert James Dr. Utley, vol. Volume 6, *Paul's Letters to a Troubled Church: I and II Corinthians*, Study Guide Commentary Series (Marshall, Texas: Bible Lessons International, 2002), 152.

[vi] Silk, Danny. Keep Your Love On: Connection Communication And Boundaries. Printopya.

[vii] Elmer, Robert. Brother Lawrence of the Resurrection. Practicing God's Presence: Brother Lawrence for Today's Reader.

[viii] Johannes P. Louw and Eugene Albert Nida, *Greek-English Lexicon of the New Testament: Based on Semantic Domains*, electronic ed. of the 2nd edition. (New York: United Bible

Societies, 1996).

ix John Ortberg, *The Life you've always wanted: Spiritual disciplines for ordinary people,* (Grand Rapids, MI: Zondervan, 2002).

x Robert James Dr. Utley, vol. Volume 6, *Paul's Letters to a Troubled Church: I and II Corinthians*, Study Guide Commentary Series (Marshall, Texas: Bible Lessons International, 2002), 153.

40316752R00099

Made in the USA
San Bernardino, CA
17 October 2016